PROTECTING
YOUR
FAMILY

PROTECTING
YOUR
FAMILY

CHARLES
STANLEY

THOMAS NELSON PUBLISHERS
Nashville

Published in Nashville, Tennessee, by Thomas Nelson, Inc.

The Bible version used in this publication is THE NEW KING JAMES VERSION. Copyright © 1979, 1980, 1982, Thomas Nelson, Inc., Publishers.

ISBN 0-7852-7282-8

Printed in the United States of America

CONTENTS

The Challenge of Protecting Your Family

The family is under attack today. A divorce in our nation is occurring every twenty-seven seconds. We face a growing drug problem and a rise in both pregnancies and AIDS among the teen population. A child runs away from home at the rate of nearly 1.3 million children a year. Even though many leaders give lip service to "family values" and the need to have strong families, the attack continues. To a great extent, the family is the number-one target of Satan.

Why is your family a target? Because your family is important to God. Your family is the primary environment in which we each learn spiritual lessons; what we hear taught at church—in Sunday school classes, sermons from the pulpit, Bible study groups—or in the Christ-centered media is what we are to *apply* at home. It is in the application of Bible-based principles that we truly *learn* how to live a godly life and to do what is pleasing to the Lord. It is in applying God's wisdom that we grow in faith and in our desire for greater intimacy with our Creator. Perhaps nothing on this earth regarding you—apart from your own personal salvation—is as important to God as your family ties.

There is a second and more global reason your family is important to God. If the family is weak, the church is weak. And if the church is weak, our nation becomes weak. There is no way that any person can be isolated unto himself or herself. In the same way, no family can be isolated from the greater community—church, neighborhood, city, state, and nation. What happens to us in our families happens to others around us to a greater or lesser degree. Your family is part of God's greater plan for the extension of His kingdom throughout the earth.

These two great reasons—your family as the place where spiritual principles are learned through application, and your family as the beginning point for all evangelism—make your family a prime target of the enemy of your soul, Satan.

Recognizing the Source of Attack

Satan uses many vehicles and methods to attack the family. Drugs and alcohol; rock music and its influence toward violence and suicide; peer pressure from ungodly children, teens, and young adults; excessive materialism; the breakdown of family togetherness; the cultural questioning of all values—each of these may be considered a source of "assault" against the family. Behind the obvious reality of these dangers, however, lies the silent, invisible, and insidious source of the attack: Satan. Regardless of what we are confronting in our families today, we must never lose sight of the fact that *Satan* is the source of all attacks against the family. He is the one who is plotting and scheming for the demise of *your* family, using whatever methods seem most readily available and effective for the individual weaknesses of your family members.

Never lose sight of your enemy as you seek to protect your family. Satan is the source of *all* evil.

It would be bad enough if Satan were attacking only the families of the unbelievers in our nation, but he has launched a major offensive against the homes of God's people. People who have been saved for years are feeling under attack. Couples who have been married ten, twenty, thirty, and more years are finding their marriages under attack.

What can we do to strengthen the home? Does the Bible have an answer for the protection and strengthening of family ties?

First, we must recognize that this is a spiritual battle. The weapons with which we defend our families against the assault of Satan are spiritual weapons. We must become not only experts in spiritual warfare, but *experienced* in spiritual warfare. We must not only know what to do in prayer, but we must actually intercede for our families. We must fight the good fight, knowing with the confidence of a firm faith that, as we do, we will win. As we act, Christ enables. As we engage in spiritual battle, Christ provides the victory.

Second, we must engage in active, positive measures that will strengthen the family against attack. Spiritual warfare is our ultimate defense against assault from Satan. But every person who has ever played any kind of sport knows that a good defense is not enough. One must also have a strong and positive offense. In the protection of our homes, that offense comes in the form of doing the "right things" to protect the family in a preventive, positive way.

The Spiritual Purpose for Protecting the Family

This study booklet deals with both a good offense and a good defense for the protection of the family. Keep in mind always, however, that the ultimate protection for your family is a spiritual matter.

The Goal

Your goal in protecting the family is spiritual—that your sons and daughters might be active, positive, strong Christians in this life and that in eternity you might stand with your sons and daughters before the throne of God and hear the Lord say to you as a family, "Well done, good and faithful servants." Nothing you do as a parent is as important as helping your children secure their spiritual and eternal future.

The Methods

Your methods for protecting the family begin in the spirit realm. It is in the teaching and applying of spiritual principles within the home that family members become strong in Christ. It is in developing spiritual warfare skills that your family members are defended against spiritual attack. It is in offering praise and thanksgiving to God that the family is encouraged during difficult times. As much as you may desire to protect your family physically, naturally, materially, financially, and relationally—all of which are necessary types of protection—the foremost protection you can supply to your family members is *spiritual* protection.

God Will Help You!

Keep in mind continually as you engage in this study that what God calls us to do, God *equips* us to do. Many people feel inadequate and even fearful at the thought of engaging in spiritual battle for their family members. Others feel inept and overwhelmed at the thought of being responsible for the spiritual education and enrichment of their children. Certainly, parenting is not for the faint of heart! Even so, what God has challenged us to do, He also will enable us to do by the power of His Holy Spirit.

You *can* be obedient in doing all that the Lord reveals to you to do. And then, you must trust God to do what only God can do. Only God can redeem, save, and fill your children with His Holy Spirit. Only God can deliver from the enemy. Only God can heal, reconcile, and make whole. We do everything we know to do, and then we must use our faith to believe that God will be faithful to His Word and work all things together for our good and the good of those we love (Rom. 8:28).

Protecting your family, in the end, is a matter of entrusting your family completely to God. You can be assured of this: God loves you and your family members even more than you do! His love is never-ending, His power is beyond measure, His wisdom is infinite. And He *will* respond to your faithful obedience.

GAINING A BIBLE PERSPECTIVE ON YOUR FAMILY

The bookshelves of countless bookstores are lined with books on family dynamics and the training of children. Many of those that are rooted in sound Christian doctrine offer good advice. Other books offer direction in spiritual warfare. Ultimately, however, the Bible is going to give every parent and spouse the *best* advice on how to protect the family against spiritual attack, and therefore, how *best* to protect the family.

All family problems ultimately have a spiritual root, and the Bible is the only book that gives God's wisdom on how to address spiritual matters. The Bible's advice regarding families is not theory—it is truth. Truth can and must be applied; it must be "lived out." The Bible not only tells us what is true and valuable, but it tells us *how* to live.

There are those who may say, "But today's world isn't like the time of the Bible. Families are different today." In some respects, families do have different concerns and constraints. The greater truth, however, is that the human heart has not and does not change. The God-ordained dynamic of family life has not and does not change. The tactics of the enemy of our souls have not and do not change. The Bible is our best source of wisdom on the human heart, human relationships, and spiritual strength and power. What the Bible has to say to you is as fresh and applicable to your life today as it has been to those in every century or millennium throughout history.

Furthermore, God's truth is not bound to any one cultural group, economic stratum, or race. The truths in God's Word are for all people. The power of God to *apply* those truths and to remain true to them is a power made possible by the Holy Spirit, who is readily given to all who have accepted Jesus Christ as Savior and seek to follow Him as Lord. No promise or principle of God related to the family is off-limits or out-of-bounds to a person's ability to receive it, act upon it, and conform to it.

As you study God's principles related to the protection of the family, I encourage you to go again and again to your Bible. Underline or highlight those phrases or verses that seem to speak in a specific or special way to you. Make notes in the margins of your Bible. I believe in a well-marked Bible—one filled with dates, notes, and insights. Take note especially of the highly personal ways in which God may admonish, encourage, or direct you to apply His Word to your life. God's truth is universal, but the application of His truth is always highly individualized to specific circumstances and situations.

For Personal or Group Study

This study guide can be used by you alone or by several people in a small-group setting. If you are using the guide for personal Bible study, you will find places from time to time in which you are asked to note your insights or respond to questions. If you are using the book for small-group study, you may use these sections for group discussion.

At various times, you will be asked to relate to the material in this guide in one of four ways:

1. What new insights have you gained?
2. Have you ever had a similar experience?
3. How do you feel about the material presented?

4. In what ways do you feel challenged to respond or to act?

Insights

Insights are not facts or opinions; rather, insights are related to the *meaning* and *application* of facts and ideas. An insight occurs when you see a truth in God's Word as if you had never seen it before. Most of us have had this experience. We may be reading a passage that we have read or studied for years, when suddenly, it's as if a light is turned on and we see something we have never seen before. In nearly all cases, what we "see" is a new nuance of meaning or a new means of applying the truth of the passage. Such insights are a genuine gift of God to you—they are given to you precisely when you need them.

Insights are generally highly individualized and often relate to an immediate or pending personal need. Insights help us make sense of that which doesn't seem to make sense; they help answer questions, give guidance to relationships, and challenge us to respond to particular experiences in ways we would not otherwise have thought to act. At still other times, insights give deep comfort or resolution to nagging doubts or spiritual questions; they bring us to a point of knowing at a deeper level *why* we believe what we believe or *how* to respond as Christ would respond.

Ask the Lord to give you insights every time you open His Word to study it. I believe He will be faithful in answering your prayer. In fact, if you haven't gained new spiritual insights after reading several passages from God's Word, you probably haven't been engaged in the process of genuine *study*. I also believe that as you have insights into God's greater truth for your life, you will have an ever-growing enthusiasm for studying His Word.

Make notes about the insights you experience. You may want to write these in your Bible or in a separate journal. The purpose for recording insights is this: when we record insights, we become very focused and intent on what it is that God is going to speak to us through His Word. The more we are *looking* for God to speak, the more He seems to speak!

At various places in this guide, you will be asked to note what a passage of the Bible is saying to you. These are times for recording your personal responses or insights, not for summarizing what others in your group may say about the passage. Make sure the insights or responses you write are your own.

Experience

No two of us have come through life to this point with exactly the same set of experiences, relationships, difficulties, victories, or environments. We each have our own bank of ideas, opinions, and emotions. Therefore, each of us has a unique perspective on what we read in God's Word.

We also tend to come to group settings with different levels of experience with God's Word. This can create problems in a group Bible study, although not in all cases. For example, those who have studied the Bible in depth and from their childhood may have a different level of understanding from that of those who have only recently come into a saving knowledge of Christ Jesus or have only recently begun to study the Bible. We must be aware of these potential differences in a group study and make certain in our discussions that the "old-timers" aren't causing beginners to feel overwhelmed, or that those who are mature in their faith aren't becoming impatient with those who are spiritual "newborns."

What we have in common are *life* experiences. We each can point to times in which we have found the Bible to be applicable to us. We can all point to experiences in which the Bible has seemed to confront, convict, challenge, encourage, or comfort us, as if that passage were written only for us.

Our experiences do not make the Bible true, of course. The Bible is truth, regardless of our input. When we share our experiences, however, we discover the many ways in which God's truth can be applied to human lives and circumstances. In sharing our life experiences, we see anew how God speaks personally and directly to each person. We learn how the Bible applies to practical needs, questions, and situations that we may not have experienced ourselves but that we *may* yet experience in life.

Sharing experiences can lead directly to spiritual growth. You will grow as you share your own experience; see this as a means of gaining courage and confidence in giving a personal witness to the power and love of God. You also will grow in understanding as you hear others share their experiences. Very often the Lord puts others in our path to share their experiences so that we will be prepared for what the future holds for us. To be forearmed with God's wisdom is a wonderful blessing when tragedy overtakes us or conflicts erupt. Be open to hearing about the faith experiences of others. Openly share what God has done in your life and how the Bible has been the foundation for your faith and a source of God's direction.

Emotional Response

Just as we each have a personal catalog of life experiences, so each of us has a set of emotional responses. Face your emotions honestly. Learn to share them openly.

Make certain that you allow others to share their emotional responses to God's Word without judgment or comment. You may be overjoyed or feel encouraged after reading a particular passage in the Bible. Another person, however, may respond to that same passage with doubt, fear, or questions.

Our families are close to our hearts, and therefore, matters that relate to the family are often highly emotional. Keep this in mind as you engage in this study. We each have a "vested interest" in the protection of our families. Be aware that we tend to be defensive when it comes to what we have or have not done as spouses, parents, or even children of older parents. Family dynamics are often very complex, and these complexities give rise to a wide range of emotions.

Those who have experienced family tragedy or conflict in the past are likely to have scars, if not open wounds. Others who are currently in the throes of a crisis or conflict are likely to have conflicting emotions: pain, anger, rejection, hurt, hate, love, forgiveness, bitterness. If the problem has existed for some time, feelings of discouragement, dejection, depression, or alienation may exist. Be sensitive to the emotions of others.

The emotional response we have to the Scriptures is directly linked to the events and experiences of our lives. At times we read a passage from the Bible with one set of emotions, at another time with another set of emotions. Our emotional responses, of course, do not give validity to the Scriptures. Nor should we trust our emotions as a measuring device for our faith. Faith is to be based on what God says, not on how a person feels. At the same time, we must recognize that our emotional response to God's Word very often impacts what we choose to *do* in the aftermath of reading God's Word. Therefore, our emotional responses are important and should be considered.

If we reject God's truth because we feel pain or conviction, we need to face up to that emotional response. If we act upon God's truth solely because we see that it is a means of making us "happy," we need to acknowledge that. If we feel paralyzed from acting because we feel fear after reading God's Word, then we need to face that issue.

There is a balance in this. Our emotions must never rule our interpretation of God's Word or cause us to limit our reading of the Bible only to those passages with which we feel comfortable. On the other hand, we must recognize that we are emotional creatures—given our emotions by God for a purpose—and that we always have an emotional response to what we believe God is saying to us.

In small-group settings, it is much more beneficial for people to express their emotions than their opinions. The Holy Spirit often speaks to us in the unspoken language of intuition, emotions, promptings, deep longings, and desires. When we share those feelings with one another, we not only open ourselves to deeper insights, but we also grow closer as members of the body of Christ; a spirit of community develops. It is as we share our joys and sorrows, doubts and assurances, hopes and fears, that we mature in sensitivity and empathy—as individuals and also as churches. We truly gain understanding in what it means to become "one in the Spirit."

Challenges

The Word of God changes our lives the more we read it. At times, this change comes through conviction—we hear God speaking to us, "Don't do this. Change your ways." At other times, the Word of God causes us to feel compelled to take a new step or to make a fresh start. We hear God saying to us through the Scriptures, "Now is a time for you to do this. Take action."

These moments of conviction or challenge can be very strong. They tend to occur repeatedly until we take action on them. They are virtually impossible to ignore or escape.

As you study ways in which to protect your family spiritually, you are likely to feel challenged or convicted at every turn. Not one of us is a "perfect person," and, therefore, not one of us is part of a perfect family. Opportunities for change and growth abound!

When you experience a time of conviction or challenge, be open to it and make sure that you get the whole of God's message to you. When we feel conviction, very often our first impulse is to close the Bible, walk away, and attempt to ignore or deny the truth of what we have read. Don't give in to that impulse! Stay in your study. Base your final decisions to take action on a complete understanding of God's principles and plan. Recognize that God is not seeking to punish you as much as He is desiring to correct you for your *future* growth and blessing. God is seeking to conform you to His plan and to cause you to mature to the full stature of Christ Jesus. Yield to His purposes!

Be aware that we are responsible to God for the ways in which He challenges *us*. So often we read God's Word and say, "Oh, now I understand what happened. It was *his* fault or it was *her* doing that resulted in a situation." The challenges that God gives us are challenges related to *us* personally and individually; they are challenges that God expects *us* to act upon. Don't become caught up in what you believe God has revealed to you about others; focus on what God is revealing to you about *you*.

I believe you can gain a great deal by writing down the ways in which God seems to be stretching you, molding you, calling you, or causing you to believe for more. When a person identifies clearly and succinctly what God desires, that person is in a much better position to make responsible and deliberate plans, and he or she is much more likely to take action and not just give lip service to a plan. We are to *respond* to God's Word, not merely react to it. Writing down the challenges we feel gives us an objectivity that allows us to respond with both faith and reason.

Ultimately, God desires to get His Word into us and us into His Word so that we can take His Word into the world. We are to live out the truth that we gain. We are to be witnesses to God's power and love in all we say and do. It is not enough for us simply to reflect upon our past experiences, record our insights, evaluate our emotional responses, or identify our challenges. We must obey God's Word and become *doers* of it (James 1:22).

Knowing how to protect your family spiritually and protecting your family spiritually are two different things. The genuine protection comes in the *doing* of the things we know to do.

Keep the Bible Central

At all times, keep the Bible central to your group study. The tendency of studies such as this, and especially so in a study related to the family, is for a group to become a therapy or support group. This book is aimed at *Bible study*. If the Bible is not kept at the center of your study, you will have no sure foundation for the sharing that you do or the prayers that you offer for one another. You will operate in human wisdom, not God's wisdom.

Certainly therapy, support, and information-sharing groups have their time and place, but ultimately, it is as we gather around God's Word—to feed upon it, learn from it, and grow into it—that we truly mature spiritually, both individually and as a family.

If you are doing a personal Bible study, you also must be diligent in staying focused on God's Word. Self-analysis and introspection are not the goals of this study. Growing into the fullness of the stature of Christ Jesus is the goal!

Prayer

I encourage you to begin and end your Bible study sessions in prayer. Ask God to give you spiritual eyes to see what He wants you to see. Ask Him to give you spiritual ears to hear His message to you. Ask Him to give you new insights, to recall to your memory the experiences that will help you grow spiritually, and to help you identify your emotions with clarity and understanding. Ask Him to reveal to you through His Word what He desires for you to do immediately or as your next step in protecting your family spiritually.

As you conclude your time of study, ask the Lord to seal to your heart and mind all that you have learned so that you will never forget it. Ask Him to transform you into the likeness of Christ, so that you might use all that you have learned and apply it in a way that is pleasing to Christ.

The Depth of God's Word

As you conclude your ten-lesson course of study, be aware that you have not "arrived" at a point of perfect protection for your family. What you have done is gained insight that will help you on your journey toward that goal. The more you continue to read and study God's Word, the more the Lord will remind you of what you have studied and point out to you new and deeper ways in which you can strengthen your family life. We never stop growing as individuals, and the same is true for our family life—we never stop growing as a family in our understanding of how to live out God's plan on this earth.

- *What new insights do you hope to gain about how to protect your family spiritually? Do you have specific needs in your family life that you are hoping will be addressed in this study?*

_____

_____

- *How do you feel about your role in protecting your family spiritually against all attacks from the enemy?*

_____

_____

- *Do you feel challenged to grow in your ability to build both a strong spiritual offense and a strong spiritual defense in your family? Are you ready to embark on that growth today?*

  _____

  _____

FOUNDATIONAL PRINCIPLES FOR A GODLY HOME

Since the attack against the home, at its root, is a spiritual attack, the key question we each must ask ourselves as parents, grandparents, aunts, and uncles is this: "How can I develop a strong *spiritual* foundation for a godly family?"

In the Gospel of Matthew, Jesus gave a teaching about the "strong man" who comes to attack a house. In this parable we find two important principles for establishing a godly home—indisputable principles upon which you can stake your family life.

Just prior to this teaching, Jesus had healed a man who was demon-possessed, blind, and mute. The man not only was delivered from Satan's power, but immediately he could both speak and see. The amazed multitudes began to ask, "Could this be the Son of David?"

To squelch any thought that Jesus might be the Messiah, a group of Pharisees accused Jesus of casting out demons by the power of Beelzebub, the ruler of the demons. Here is what Jesus said in reply to their accusation:

Jesus knew their thoughts, and said to them: "Every kingdom divided against itself is brought to desolation, and every city or house divided against itself will not stand. If Satan casts out Satan, he is divided against himself. How then will his kingdom stand? And if I cast out demons by Beelzebub, by whom do your sons cast them out? Therefore they shall be your judges. But if I cast out demons by the Spirit of God, surely the kingdom of God has come upon you. Or how can one enter a strong man's house and plunder his goods, unless he first binds the strong man? And then he will plunder his house. (Matt. 12:25–29)

Jesus made these two points very clear in His response to the Pharisees:

1. Division brings about destruction.
2. God is greater than any satanic power.

Division Brings Desolation

First, Jesus said, "Every kingdom divided against itself is brought to desolation, and every city or house divided against itself will not stand" (Matt. 12:25).

We see that principle at work all around us. If a church becomes divided—some of the people holding one opinion, some another—the church will become splintered or "split," and if that breach continues, grows, and is not healed, the church may eventually disintegrate and disband.

The division initially may not be over anything that is all that earthshaking. It's not the *reason* for the division that brings about the desolation; rather, it is the fact that the people have allowed themselves to become divided.

The same thing happens in the home. If a husband and wife or a parent and child become divided, the home as a whole will feel that division, and it will be fractured, weakened, and ultimately may experience a "split," even to the point of separation, estrangement and alienation, and perhaps divorce or the "disowning" of a child by a parent or a parent by a child.

The most potent means of destroying any organization, institution, or entity is *internal strife* or internal conflict. An undivided, unified family, church, or other institution of society can withstand virtually any external onslaught. But an internal conflict brings about distrust, division, and disintegration.

Jesus said, "If Satan casts out Satan, he is divided against himself. How then will his kingdom stand?" (Matt. 12:26). In other words, Jesus argued, "If you are accusing me of doing miracles by Satan, then Satan is actually working against himself—he is put into a position of both healing and destroying. That simply isn't possible."

- *In your life experiences, can you cite an incident in which division brought about a feeling of desolation or destruction?*

_____

_____

- *How does it feel to be divided or "separated" from another person you love or with whom you were once in close fellowship?*

_____

_____

Inner Division

The division we experience usually begins as an "inner conflict" or a "divided mind." A person begins to hold a thought, feeling, or opinion that is *contrary* to God's absolute commandments or desires. The exact opposite of this state is to be "one in the Spirit," to hold fast to the central truth of God's Word and to what God desires for us to do, say, and be. The godhead—Father, Son, and Holy Spirit—is our great example of unity. Jesus never did anything that was not something He first "saw" His heavenly Father do. The Spirit flows from the Father and the Son in complete harmony. In like manner, we are called to discern the will of God and then do it. As we each come to a full understanding of God's will, we *can* experience unity in the Spirit. We may still have differences of personality and style, but our choices regarding behavior and the commitment of our will are to be rooted in God's absolutes.

What the Word Says	What the Word Says to Me
Their heart is divided;	------------------------------
Now they are held guilty.	------------------------------
He will break down their altars;	------------------------------
He will ruin their sacred pillars.	------------------------------
For now they say,	------------------------------
"We have no king,	------------------------------
Because we did not fear the LORD.	------------------------------
And as for a king, what would he	------------------------------
do for us?"	------------------------------
They have spoken words,	------------------------------
Swearing falsely in making a	------------------------------
covenant.	------------------------------
Thus judgment springs up like	------------------------------
hemlock in the	------------------------------
furrows of the field. (Hos. 10:2–4)	------------------------------
There is neither Jew nor Greek,	------------------------------
there is neither slave nor free,	------------------------------
there is neither male nor female;	------------------------------
for you are all one in Christ Jesus.	------------------------------
(Gal. 3:28)	------------------------------
Only let your conduct be worthy	------------------------------
of the gospel of Christ . . . that you	------------------------------
stand fast in one spirit, with one	------------------------------
mind striving together for the	------------------------------
faith of the gospel. (Phil. 1:27)	------------------------------

Satan *Cannot* Produce Good

Throughout the Scriptures, "division" among God's people—including a division in the home, as well as a division in belief against the law of God—is associated with negative situations and outcomes. It was when Israel became divided, northern tribes against southern tribes, that the empire built by David and Solomon collapsed. It was when the Israelites rebelled against God and became divided in their attempt to serve both God and false gods that great calamity befell them. Much of Paul's and Peter's teachings about submission is rooted in the understanding that unity and harmony are to prevail over division and disharmony.

In confronting the Pharisees, Jesus was not only saying that division brings desolation, but that Satan simply isn't capable of bringing about anything that is *good*. Satan's purposes against the family are always its destruction. Nothing that he does with regard to the family is for the good of the family, although many of the things that he uses as temptations may *seem* to be for the family's good.

For example, Satan seems to be tempting many families these days by saying, "It's important that parents spend time with their children. Since time is of such great value, it's more important that parents spend time with their children on Sunday mornings and Sunday evenings than for those parents to bring their children to church." Satan's temptation is that parents spend time with their children at home rather than at church and that the net result will be of a greater good to the family.

Not so! It is the family that prays together and worships together that stays united in faith—not the family that watches cartoons together or plays tennis together on Sunday mornings. Giving into a temptation to stay away from church brings about a "division" between a family and the church as a whole.

As another example, Satan may tempt a father or mother by saying, "You could do so much more for your children and for your family as a whole if you just used the money that you now give to the church for your children instead."

Not so! Giving to God what rightfully belongs to God sends a message to children of obedience, discipline, and God-centered priorities. Those values are weakened greatly when a parent says to a child, in effect, "Your pair of designer jeans is more important than giving to the church" or "Buying you a new car is more valuable than giving to missions, which can result in the salvation of souls." The end result of such thinking is a divided mind about material and financial priorities.

The temptations of Satan always appear good in principle, but underneath, they are deadly and divisive to one's faith.

• *Can you recall a time in which you were of a "divided mind"
about something? How did you feel? What happened?*

_____

_____

God's Power Is Greater

Second, Jesus said to the Pharisees, "If I cast out demons by
Beelzebub, by whom do your sons cast them out? Therefore they
shall be your judges" (Matt. 12:27).

A number of Jews attempted to cast out demons using a variety
of exorcism methods that had been "sanctioned" by the Pharisees.
Jesus argued, "If it is casting out demons that is under question
here, then what about those who are casting out demons under
your authority?" Jesus put them into a position of defending themselves.

Jesus went on, "But if I cast out demons by the Spirit of God,
surely the kingdom of God has come upon you" (Matt. 12:28).

The principle is this: God has the power to *cast out* demons. Satan
may have authority over his own demons, but he does not have
absolute authority over them. In other words, Satan cannot rescue
his demons from the greater power of God. Believers in Christ Jesus
can cast out demons in the name of Jesus and by the power of the
Holy Spirit. The ultimate authority over evil is God.

Many Christians seem confused on that point today. They seem
to think that Satan's power is just as potent as God's power—only
toward the negative. That is not what the Bible teaches. God's power
is absolute. He is *omnipotent—all*-powerful. God has authority over
Satan. His power cannot even be compared to Satan's power. God
has *allowed* Satan to have a limited degree of influence on this earth
as a part of giving mankind free will. Satan has the power to tempt
and to oppress. But all of Satan's power must be confined to the
limits that God puts upon him.

What does this mean to us today with regard to our families?
It means that when we rely upon God, through His Son, Jesus Christ,
we are tapping into a power source that is greater than evil power.

The Word of God against Satan in our families is stronger than the word of the devil whispered in the ears of the unsuspecting and weak.

For Jesus to have healed a man who was demon-possessed, blind, and mute, Jesus had to be stronger than the powers that were holding this man in his bondage.

What the Word Says

Beloved, do not believe every spirit, but test the spirits, whether they are of God; because many false prophets have gone out into the world. By this you know the Spirit of God: Every spirit that confesses that Jesus Christ has come in the flesh is of God, and every spirit that does not confess that Jesus Christ has come in the flesh is not of God. And this is the spirit of the Antichrist, which you have heard was coming, and is now already in the world. You are of God, little children, and have overcome them, because He who is in you is greater than he who is in the world. (1 John 4:1–4)

Then I heard a loud voice saying in heaven, "Now salvation, and strength, and the kingdom of our God, and the power of His Christ have come, for the accuser of our brethren, who accused them before our God day and night, has been cast down. And they overcame him by the blood of the Lamb and by the word of their testimony, and they did not love their lives to the death. (Rev. 12:10–11)

What the Word Says to Me

_____

_____

_____

_____

_____

_____

_____

_____

_____

_____

_____

_____

_____

_____

_____

_____

_____

_____

_____

_____

_____

_____

_____

_____

_____

_____

_____

The Greater Power of Love

One of the greatest powers that God has given us for *good* is the power to love.

Those who truly love—and who choose to love regardless of circumstance or situation—are powerful forces for God and for good. What we say in love brings about *good* things. What we do out of unconditional love brings about *good* situations and relationships. God honors all that we say and do when we are motivated by love for Him and love for others, even if we make mistakes and err at times in *how* we show our love. Never be afraid to love others. Your expression of love will ultimately result in both harmony and a defeat of Satan.

It is out of genuine love for our families that we each are called to come to the position of saying: "I choose to love my family, and I will not allow us to be divided. We *will* come to know God and to base our lives upon His Word. We *will* become one in the Spirit."

It is out of love that we are to combat the forces of evil that come our way, in effect declaring to the spirit realm, "I love my family to the point that I will lay down my very life if necessary to see Satan defeated in their lives."

Love must become the number-one motivating force behind our desire to have a strong family. Without love, we simply will not pay the price of denying self, which is required if we are to live in unity and harmony with one another. Without love, we will not pay the price of time, energy, and spiritual purity required to engage in spiritual warfare on one another's behalf. Every family I know can use more love—both love of God and love for one another. It is when we fail to love that we fail to desire agreement and we fail to experience victory over the enemy of our souls and our families.

Our love is always to be a reflection of God's love and of God's goodness. It is out of God's goodness that He loves. It is out of God's presence within us that we have the capacity and the courage to love.

Any time we are confronted with a situation that seems to have the potential to "tear us apart," we must turn to God and say, "Let me experience more of Your love." It is love that ultimately heals division and brings about harmony in Christ.

- *Have you ever had an experience in which a genuine expression of love overcame differences of opinions or hurt feelings so that unity was restored to a relationship?*

_____

_____

What the Word Says

If someone says, "I love God," and hates his brother, he is a liar; for he who does not love his brother whom he has seen, how can he love God whom he has not seen? And this commandment we have from Him: that he who loves God must love his brother also. (1 John 4:20–21)

By this we know that we love the children of God, when we love God and keep His commandments. For this is the love of God, that we keep His commandments. (1 John 5:2–3)

This is My commandment, that you love one another as I have loved you. Greater love has no one than this, than to lay down one's life for his friends. (John 15:12–13)

What the Word Says to Me

_____

_____

_____

_____

- *What new insights do you have into God's Word about how to develop a strong foundation for the family?*

_____

_____

- *In what ways are you feeling challenged today to build a firmer foundation for YOUR family?*

_____

_____

LESSON 3

STEWARDSHIP OF THE FAMILY

So often we think of stewardship as relating only to the giving of our time, talents, and resources to God and the church. Stewardship, however, is a much broader concept. It refers to the "caretaking" of anything that God has given to us. Certainly that is a concept that relates to our families!

Family Is a Gift from God

Two central principles of God related to stewardship have a direct bearing on the family:

1. Our children and families are *entrusted* to us as a highly valuable gift from God, and we are commanded to care for those things that God gives us.
2. We must give an account for our stewardship of our families.

God's Gift

Our families are God's gift to us. Every child is a gift from God. How much stronger our commitment to family would be if we truly saw our families from God's perspective and *cared* for our families as our most treasured possession.

Many parents today seem to think of their children more as a burden than a gift. They see their children as "costing" them their freedom, interfering with their careers, or being a burden to them financially. Sadly, a child "feels" these attitudes. Even if you have never voiced to your children a feeling that they are a burden to you, if that is the true feeling of your heart, your children will *know* how you feel.

Those who consider their children to be a burden are likely to reject their children. Consider the impact the three statements below have upon a child:

1. "Get out of my way" (perhaps adding, "while I'm working" or "while I'm fixing dinner").
2. "I don't have time for you right now."
3. "You can't do this—let me do it."

Each of these statements sends a message to a child, "Stay away from me because you are a burden to me" or "You hinder me." Certainly our heavenly Father *never* treats us that way when we come to Him. He always has time for us, wants to be involved with us, and allows us to be a part of His work on this earth—even if we aren't perfect and don't do things perfectly. God never rejects us. And in like manner, we are never to reject our children or a spouse. To do so is to fail to see that person as a gift of God to your life.

• *Have you ever been rejected by a person who seemed to see you more as a burden than a "gift"? How did you feel?*

_____

_____

Eve, the mother of all living, declared when she gave birth to Cain, "I have acquired a man from the LORD" (Gen. 4:1). Eve clearly perceived that her son was a gift from God—not an accident of nature, not an ill-timed conception, not a deed of man. This is the proper perspective we each are to have of our children. They are God's creation, entrusted to us as His *gift*.

We Are Accountable

Furthermore, God holds us accountable for all that He entrusts to us. This is not only true of the material and financial blessings we receive, but of the great blessing of family. Read this familiar parable of Jesus with your *family* in mind:

> For the kingdom of heaven is like a man traveling to a far country, who called his own servants and delivered his goods to them. And to one he gave five talents, to another two, and to another one, to each according to his own ability; and immediately he went on a journey. . . . After a long time the lord of those servants came and settled accounts with them. So he who had received five talents came and brought five other talents, saying, "Lord, you delivered to me five talents; look, I have gained five more talents besides them." His lord said to him, "Well done, good and faithful servant; you were faithful over a few things, I will make you ruler over many things. Enter into the joy of your lord." He also who had received two talents came and said, "Lord, you delivered to me two talents; look, I have gained two more talents besides them." His lord said to him, "Well done, good and faithful servant; you have been faithful over a few things, I will make you ruler over many things. Enter into the joy of your lord." Then he who had received the one talent came and said, "Lord, I knew you to be a hard man, reaping where you have not sown, and gathering where you have not scattered seed. And I was afraid, and went and hid your talent in the ground. Look, there you have what is yours." But his lord answered and said to him, "You wicked and lazy servant, you knew that I reap where I have not sown, and gather where I have not scattered seed. . . . Therefore take the talent from him, and give it to him who has ten talents. For to everyone who has, more will be given, and he will have abundance." (Matt. 25:14–15, 19–26, 28–29)

• *What new insights do you have into this passage of Scripture?*

_____

_____

Now certainly we aren't to "trade" our children or to "bury" them; furthermore, God does not "take" our children from us and give them to others. But note these strong teachings about our children that we can draw from this parable:

First, God gives us our children so that we might "develop" them. We are responsible for seeing that the hidden talents of our children are brought to light and developed. We are also called to build up our children and to "multiply" within them their self-esteem and confidence.

This does not happen when we say to our children:

- "Can't you ever do anything right?"
- "I don't think you'll ever amount to anything."
- "Why can't you be more like your brother [or sister]?"
- "You are an embarrassment to me."
- "We never wanted you in the first place."

Statements such as those do anything *but* build up a child! To a great degree, they "bury" a child in a pit of self-depreciation and low esteem.

Second, God holds us accountable for the way we treat our children. He will ask us when we stand before Him in heaven, "Where is your child?" God's number-one expectation of us is that we will raise our children to love and serve Him and to be faithful followers of His Word . . . all the way into eternity!

Third, God enlarges our personal witness to others on the basis of how we treat our family members. Our families are to be our number-one mission field. It is to our families that we are to show God's love and to express our faith in God. As we treat our family members, so God allows our witness and ministry to be effective to others outside our family. The man or woman who cannot show God's love at home is a person whom God cannot trust fully to show His love to the world.

- *In what ways are you feeling challenged today in your role within the family?*

_____

_____

What the Word Says	What the Word Says to Me
Behold, children are a heritage from the LORD, The fruit of the womb is a reward. (Ps. 127:3)	----------------------------- ----------------------------- ----------------------------- -----------------------------
[Jesus taught], "Whoever receives one little child like this in My name receives Me. But whoever causes one of these little ones who believe in Me to sin, it would be better for him if a millstone were hung around his neck, and he were drowned in the depth of the sea." (Matt. 18:5–6)	----------------------------- ----------------------------- ----------------------------- ----------------------------- ----------------------------- ----------------------------- ----------------------------- ----------------------------- -----------------------------
[Jesus said], "For everyone to whom much is given, from him much will be required; and to whom much has been committed, of him they will ask the more." (Luke 12:48)	----------------------------- ----------------------------- ----------------------------- ----------------------------- ----------------------------- -----------------------------

Every child needs to grow up knowing:

- "You *are* somebody! You have been gifted and blessed by God in unique and wonderful ways."
- "You *count;* you are important to God and to me, your parent. God has a special place for you in His kingdom."
- "You have a great capacity to bring glory to God."
- "You are wanted by me and by God. I will do my best to care for you on this earth and to lead you to a lasting faith in Christ. God has an eternal home for you in heaven, and He is with you always to care for you, protect you, and to provide for you. He loves you and desires to forgive you to bring you to a full relationship with Him through Christ Jesus."

What the Word Says	What the Word Says to Me
[Jesus said]: "Judge not, and you shall not be judged. Condemn not, and you shall not be condemned. Forgive, and you will be forgiven." (Luke 6:37)	------------------------------- ------------------------------- ------------------------------- ------------------------------- -------------------------------
[Jesus said]: "And whenever you stand praying, if you have anything against anyone, forgive him, that your Father in heaven may also forgive you your trespasses. But if you do not forgive, neither will your Father in heaven forgive your trespasses." (Mark 11:25–26)	------------------------------- ------------------------------- ------------------------------- ------------------------------- ------------------------------- ------------------------------- ------------------------------- ------------------------------- -------------------------------

Make these the messages you give to your children today. They are messages strongly rooted in God's love. They are messages that build a relationship with Christ. A child who grows up having these truths taught on a daily basis in the home is a child who is not only confident in himself, but a child who is assured of God's greatness and goodness. Such a child *will* bless the world.

Your Child Will Do What You Do

Your child will care for himself in the same way that you care for your child. He will "model" your behavior. This is a vital principle for you to see in your stewardship of your family. We each must not only be "speakers" of the truth to our children, but "doers" of the truth. What your child sees you do, your child will do.

As you value yourself and your relationship to other family members, so your child will value his relationship to you and to others. As you value yourself and your relationship with God, so your child will come to value his relationship with God.

Jesus taught that none of us can be "greater" than those who teach us (John 13:16). Your child, therefore, is not likely to be a better parent or a better Christian than you are (unless he has a teacher or role model later in life who is highly influential). You are responsible for teaching your child how to respond to life in a godly manner. That is what has been entrusted to you. That is what God holds you accountable for doing!

You are entrusted with teaching *by example* those things that are of greatest value in life: how to love God and others, how to have faith in God, how to live in daily relationship with the Holy Spirit. You are accountable for teaching your child these lessons.

Teaching as You Go

What we teach our children must be rooted in daily experience. Deuteronomy 6:6–7 says, "These words which I command you today shall be in your heart. You shall teach them diligently to your children, and shall talk of them when you sit in your house, when you walk by the way, when you lie down, and when you rise up." We are to teach our children *as* we are in the home and as we go about our daily work and responsibilities, from dawn to dusk. The lessons we teach our children are to be rooted in *daily life*. They are to be practical lessons—God's truth in *action*.

In the end, stewardship is not something we do primarily with our words. It is something that we do first and foremost with our deeds.

What the Word Says	What the Word Says to Me
But be doers of the word, and not hearers only, deceiving yourselves. For if anyone is a hearer of the word and not a doer, he is like a man observing his natural face in a mirror; for he observes himself, goes away, and immediately forgets what kind of man he was. But he who looks into the perfect law of liberty and continues in it, and is not a forgetful hearer but a doer of the work, this one will be blessed in what he does. (James 1:22–25)	_____ _____ _____ _____ _____ _____ _____ _____ _____ _____ _____ _____ _____

[Jesus said], "I have given you an example, that you should do as I have done to you. Most assuredly, I say to you, a servant is not greater than his master; nor is he who is sent greater than he who sent him. If you know these things, blessed are you if you do them." (John 13:15–17)

The "Role Model" We Give Our Children

As parents we are entrusted with the responsibility for modeling two sets of behaviors to our children:

- We are to be role models of both a marital and a parental role. (Family Relationship Role Model)
- We are to be role models of a "Christian in action." (Spiritual Role Model)

You are responsible for teaching your child what it means to be a husband or a wife, and also what it means to be a parent. Nobody can or will teach these lessons as well as you do! Long after your child is grown, a "tape" of your example will play in your child's mind, saying, "This is how I should respond to my spouse. This is how I should act as a parent."

You are also responsible for teaching your child *how* to be a Christian—not only what it means to believe in Christ Jesus, but what it means to have a daily walk of obedience to God's Word. God has entrusted you to teach these lessons well and in full accordance with His Word!

Marital Roles

The Bible states very clearly the basics for being a good spouse and parent. In Ephesians 5:22–33 we read,

Wives, submit to your own husbands, as to the Lord. For the husband is head of the wife, as also Christ is head of the church; and He is the Savior of the body. Therefore, just as the church is subject to Christ, so let the wives be to their own husbands in everything. Husbands, love your wives, just as Christ also loved the church and gave Himself for her, that He might sanctify and cleanse her with the washing of water by the word, that He might present her to Himself a glorious church, not having spot or wrinkle or any such thing, but that she should be holy and without blemish. So husbands ought to love their own wives as their own bodies; he who loves his wife loves himself. For no one ever hated his own flesh, but nourishes and cherishes it, just as the Lord does the church. For we are members of His body, of His flesh and of His bones. "For this reason a man shall leave his father and mother and be joined to his wife, and the two shall become one flesh." This is a great mystery, but I speak concerning Christ and the church. Nevertheless let each one of you in particular so love his own wife as himself, and let the wife see that she respects her husband.

• *What new insights do you have into this passage of Scripture as it relates to the* stewardship *of your family and the lessons you are entrusted to teach your children?*

_____

_____

Note these specifics:

Wives are to love and respect their husbands as they love and respect Christ Jesus. They are to be helpmeets to their husbands in all aspects of life.

Husbands are to love, provide for, protect, and "serve" their wives, just as Christ loves, provides for, protects, and serves us—even to the laying down of His life.

Husbands are to be the spiritual decision makers or "heads" of the family, even as they take their "marching orders" from God. Wives are to submit to their husbands in this, just as the church submits to God.

In all ways, Christ is to be our model and our behavior toward one another as spouses is to reflect His relationship to the church.

Through the years, I have counseled a number of young people who were raised in a home where the father was passive and the mother was domineering—in other words, homes in which the roles described above were reversed. What has been the result in the lives of the children? I've seen mental illness, including a great deal of schizophrenia, eating disorders, self-abusive behaviors and addictions, and depression. I've witnessed in these young people homosexuality and other forms of perverse sexual behavior, including promiscuity and pornography. I've seen young people who reenact a pattern of marital discord in their own families.

We cannot improve upon God's "order" for husband and wife relationships. We can, however, obey God's commandments in this and see healthy, fruitful behavior in our children!

- *How do you feel about the roles that God has prescribed for husbands and wives?*

  _____

  _____

- *In what ways are you feeling challenged today?*

  _____

  _____

Parental Role Modeling

As a parent, you are to act in such a way that you "do not provoke your children to wrath, but bring them up in the training and admonition of the Lord" (Eph. 6:4).

The best way *not* to provoke a child to wrath (or to angry behavior rooted in bitterness) is to both show and tell a child how much you love him or her. Don't be hesitant or stingy in telling your child, "I love you." Every child needs to hear that message often, no matter how old the child may be. Don't withhold your hugs and tender kisses. A child needs to know that you value a "closeness" of relationship. (At all times, of course, we are to be pure and chaste in our touching relationship with a child.)

I have often asked teens who have become involved in immorality, "Tell me about your father." Not one has ever said to me, "My dad really loved me." Fathers especially need to learn how to express love to their children—both in verbal and nonverbal ways. Your child needs to experience the warmth of your feelings!

A child who truly grows up feeling the unconditional love of a parent is a child who will, in turn, express that love to others—including his or her own child someday.

- *Did you know the warmth of a parent's affection as a child? In what ways do you feel challenged to express a warmth of love—both verbally and nonverbally—to your own children?*

  _____

  _____

- *In what ways do you feel challenged today?*

  _____

  _____

Modeling the Christian Life

Paul wrote that we are to bring up our children in the "training and admonition" of the Lord (Eph. 6:4). In other words, we are to teach them Christian disciplines. To train is to teach by *doing*. Training does not involve theory alone—it requires *practice*. To "admonish" your child in the Lord is to require your child to engage in Christian practice. Even though your child may not have a great depth of meaning for various Christian disciplines—such as prayer, attending church, reading the Bible, giving—your child does have the capability to *practice* these disciplines, and over time, to acquire more and more meaning related to them.

Paul wrote to Timothy, "But you must continue in the things which you have learned and been assured of, knowing from whom you have learned them, and that from childhood you have known the Holy Scriptures, which are able to make you wise for salvation through faith which is in Christ Jesus" (2 Tim. 3:14–15).

As parents, we are to teach *by our examples* what we value to be true about:

- Money
- The Bible
- Prayer
- Friends
- Self
- The church
- Government and those in authority
- Personal freedom and liberty
- A walk of faith in the Lord
- God's servants
- Others who don't know the Lord
- Family members (immediate and extended)

Children, of course, are quick to spot hypocrisy. What we say we believe, we must *do*. For example, your child will be quick to observe any difference that may exist between what you say about money and how you handle money, including the tithe and gifts you give to the church. A child will note immediately if you value church attendance or involvement with other believers. We each must be consistent in our behavior.

If you want your child to grow up attending church, then attend church faithfully as a family.

If you want your child to have a strong prayer life, then pray often with your child. Let him learn how to pray by hearing you pray.

If you want your child to learn how to relate in a loving way to those in the church, including those in church leadership and those outside the church to whom the ministry of the church is extended, let your child accompany you as you help with various church activities and as you participate in outreach ministries.

If you want your child to grow up knowing the Bible and following its teachings, then you must not only read the Bible with your child but let your child see that you are studying the Bible and attempting to apply its truth to your life on a daily basis.

What your child sees you do and what your child is *included in doing with you* will be what your child later does as an adult.

Above all, model forgiveness to your child. Be quick to say, "I'm sorry" or to admit, "I was wrong" and to ask your child, "Please forgive me." The child who grows up with a strong role model in this area will be a child who is quick to make amends with others and quick to seek God's forgiveness for his own sin.

What the Word Says	What the Word Says to Me
We cannot but speak the things which we have seen and heard. (Acts 4:20)	_____ _____ _____
The things which you learned and received and heard and saw in me, these do, and the God of peace will be with you. (Phil. 4:9)	_____ _____ _____ _____
That which was from the beginning, which we have heard, which we have seen with our eyes, which we have looked upon, and our hands have handled, concerning the Word of life . . . we declare to you, that you also may have fellowship with us; and truly our fellowship is with the Father and with His Son Jesus Christ. (1 John 1:1, 3)	_____ _____ _____ _____ _____ _____ _____ _____ _____ _____

- *What new insights do you have into your role as a "steward" of your family?*

  _____

  _____

- *In what ways do you feel challenged today regarding the stewardship of your family before the Lord?*

  _____

  _____

LOVING YOUR FAMILY UNCONDITIONALLY

Few things do as much for a person as unconditional love!

Unconditional love is one of the greatest gifts you can ever give to another person. Love is the message underlying the gospel: "For God so *loved* the world that He *gave* His only begotten Son" (John 3:16). When you truly love another person, you will be motivated not only to share the gospel of Jesus Christ with that person, but to *live* the gospel in your relationship with the person. Love compels us to keep God's commandments so that our relationships with God and other people might become deeper and more fulfilling. Love is the proper motivation for giving and forgiving. Love received from God and others causes us to blossom and become all that God has ordained for us to be.

Unconditional love is a "regardless" love—we choose to love regardless of another person's dress, hairstyle, choice of music . . . indeed, regardless of *any* behavior the person might display. We love regardless of the other person's successes or failures in life. We love regardless of what another person says or does to us. Genuine unconditional love is love with no "ifs" or other qualifiers. It is love rooted solely in the fact that we choose to love.

Unconditional love is impossible without first having a sense that you are loved. Whether your parents did or did not give you that kind of love, it is vitally important that you receive God's unconditional love. As John tells us, "We love Him because He first loved us" (1 John 4:19).

- *In your life, how have you experienced unconditional love?*

_____

_____

What the Word Says	What the Word Says to Me
God is love, and he who abides in love abides in God, and God in him. (1 John 4:16)	_____ _____ _____
Love has been perfected among us in this: that we may have boldness in the day of judgment; because as He is, so are we in this world. There is no fear in love; but perfect love casts out fear. (1 John 4:17–18)	_____ _____ _____ _____ _____ _____
Whoever believes that Jesus is the Christ is born of God, and everyone who loves Him who begot also loves him who is begotten of Him. (1 John 5:1)	_____ _____ _____ _____ _____
My little children, let us not love in word or in tongue, but in deed and in truth. (1 John 3:18)	_____ _____ _____

How Do We Show Unconditional Love?

In a previous lesson, we discussed the great importance of love for your family. In this lesson, we will deal with the practicalities of loving your family unconditionally. Our key question is this, "*How* might we show unconditional love to our family members?"

First, unconditional love causes us to want to know others as unique and wonderful creations of God. One of the foremost ways you can show love to your spouse or your child is to make a diligent effort to understand your spouse or child. Peter admonished husbands to take this attitude toward their wives: "Dwell with them with understanding" (1 Peter 3:7).

Every person is a beloved and one-of-a-kind creation by God. Each person has been given specific gifts, talents, desires, abilities, and callings. When we recognize the uniqueness of those in our family, we should stand in awe of God's creativity. He has made each person special in wonderful ways.

Unconditional love says, "I am glad God made you the way you are and has placed you into my life." Our thanksgiving is to God; our appreciation is to Him.

Certainly we are to discern between good and evil and between right and wrong behaviors. Behaviors are learned, and they can be relearned. We must guard ourselves against accepting willful behavior as a "given" by God. As much as we discern willful behavior, however, we are also to discern the wonderful inherent and God-given traits of a person—those characteristics that truly make the person himself or herself. These are things that cannot be changed (within limits)—they can only be *developed* and *used*.

In showing God's unconditional love to others, we are wise to help them discover their own talents, develop them, and use them for God's glory. That is the role that parents are privileged to play in the lives of their children: see your child as God sees your child and help your child fulfill his or her God-ordained destiny.

- *How do you feel about being a unique and beloved creation of God?*

  _____

  _____

- *In what ways are you being challenged to extend this same recognition to others in your family?*

  _____

  _____

What the Word Says

Then God saw everything that He had made, and indeed it was very good. (Gen. 1:31)

For I know the thoughts that I think toward you, says the LORD, thoughts of peace and not of evil, to give you a future and a hope. (Jer. 29:11)

What the Word Says to Me

Second, as a part of knowing and loving others, we are called to listen to others intently. One of the ways we show unconditional love to our spouse and children is to listen to them fully—to listen with interest and not out of obligation, to listen to them regardless of what it is that they desire to communicate to us, to listen because we value them as individuals. Certainly God loves us this way. He is always available to us when we pray; no subject is off-limits with Him. We only have to read the Psalms to see that the psalmist felt very free in pouring out all of his emotions and opinions to God—nothing was held back! In fact, David referred to God as "You who hear prayer" (Ps. 65:2).

We show love to our family members when we choose to hear them as God hears them—any time of day or night, regardless of situation or circumstance, never considering their conversation to be an interruption or an annoyance.

A child or spouse who has a full opportunity for expression without condemnation, and who knows that he is being heard to the best of the listener's ability to listen, is a person who feels wanted, valued, and in relationship. The child or spouse who is not heard fully is a person who feels unimportant, unloved, and who questions the validity of the relationship.

A study done at the University of Michigan showed that working mothers spend only about eleven minutes a day of "quality time" with their children, and working fathers only about eight minutes a day. Of this time, only about half of it is spent listening to a child. The time spent on weekend days was only thirty minutes for mothers and fourteen minutes for fathers. That simply isn't enough listening time if you want to express love to your child!

In listening intently to your family members,

- look them in the eye, face-to-face,
- don't interrupt or change the subject,
- ask questions and do your best to answer their questions, and
- seek out their opinions regarding family-related decisions.

Remember always that it is not how *we* perceive ourselves as listeners that counts; it is how our family members perceive us as listeners. Spend time with your spouse and children; listen to what they have to say with the intent of understanding them better.

- *How does it feel to talk to someone whom you know is hearing but not truly listening to you—their mind is on something else?*

_____

_____

- *In what ways are you feeling challenged to show love to your family members?*

_____

_____

What the Word Says

I will extol You, O LORD, for You have lifted me up,
And have not let my foes rejoice over me.
O LORD my God, I cried out to You,
And You healed me. (Ps. 30:1–2)

The LORD has heard the voice of my weeping.

What the Word Says to Me

_____

_____

_____

_____

_____

_____

_____

_____

_____

The LORD has heard my supplica-
tion;
The LORD will receive my prayer.
(Ps. 6:8–9)

The hearing ear and the seeing
eye,
The LORD has made them both.
(Prov. 20:12)

Third, we must not let the "performance" or behavior of a spouse or child influence our love. Unconditional love is given without regard to whether the goal was reached, the touchdown was scored, the "A" was earned, or the dinner was perfectly cooked. Conditional love, in comparison, is based upon the philosophy of "I will love you if you do what I *expect* or *require* you to do."

God's blessings and chastisements are based upon our performance in keeping His commandments, but His love and forgiveness are never based upon performance! His love is motivated solely by His desire to love. The same must be true for us. We can reward or chastise our children based upon their performance in keeping certain family rules, but we must never withhold our love, *regardless* of behavior.

Consider two of the best things you can do for your child:

1. Challenge your child to do his or her personal best rather than strive to achieve group-related norms or goals.
2. Seek out activities that are at the level of your child's ability so that your child has a good opportunity to succeed at what he or she attempts.

God never gave His people laws or commandments that were beyond their ability to keep. He always *expected* them to keep His laws—they were well within human ability to perform. Furthermore, God always calls us to be our moral best. He challenges us to excel in righteousness and faithfulness, not necessarily to be a success in the eyes of others.

- *How does it feel when others love you regardless of your mistakes or poor performance?*

_____

_____

- *In what ways are you feeling challenged to show love to your family members?*

_____

_____

The Bible teaches that *nothing* can separate us from God's love. In Romans 8:35 we read, "Who shall separate us from the love of Christ? Shall tribulation, or distress, or persecution, or famine, or nakedness, or peril, or sword?" The answer Paul gives is a resounding no! We must have this same stance regarding our family: that no outside situation, circumstance, problem, crisis, or need will be allowed to quench the love we have for our family. No matter the behavior problem that may exist in the life of a family member, you must not let that problem separate you or divide you in your love. In fact, unconditional love is very likely one of the strongest factors that will help you and your family members overcome behavioral problems by seeking out godly solutions!

What the Word Says

Now it shall come to pass, if you diligently obey the voice of the LORD your God, to observe carefully all His commandments which I command you today, that the LORD your God will set you high above all nations of the earth. And all these blessings shall come upon you and overtake you, because you obey the voice of the LORD your God. (Deut. 28:1–2)

The LORD has appeared of old to me, saying:

What the Word Says to Me

_____

_____

_____

_____

_____

_____

_____

_____

_____

_____

_____

_____

"Yes, I have loved you with an
everlasting love;
Therefore with lovingkindness I
have drawn you." (Jer. 31:3)

[Jesus said], "As the Father loved
Me, I also have loved you; abide in
My love." (John 15:9)

Unconditional Love Leads Us to Forgive

It is out of unconditional love that we truly are able to forgive others, regardless of the offense or sin against us. Even when we are faced with hatred, anger, bitterness, or rejection, we are capable of forgiving if we truly have unconditional love in our hearts.

Jesus taught very clearly, "Forgive, and you will be forgiven" (Luke 6:37). Furthermore, He taught that it is *only* as we forgive others that we are capable of receiving God's full forgiveness for our own sins (Mark 11:25–26).

Unconditional love and a quickness to forgive others go hand in hand. If we withhold forgiveness, we are saying to others, "My love for you is related to what you do and don't do." That is conditional love, not unconditional love. Withholding forgiveness brings about a feeling of shame; shame and love are never compatible!

- *How do you feel when another person is quick to forgive you for the wrongs you have done against him?*

- *In what ways are you feeling challenged to show love to your family?*

What the Word Says

[Jesus said], "But if you love those
who love you, what credit is that

What the Word Says to Me

to you? For even sinners love those who love them." (Luke 6:32)

[Jesus said], "Whenever you stand praying, if you have any-thing against anyone, forgive him, that your Father in heaven may also forgive you your trespasses. But if you do not forgive, neither will your Father in heaven forgive your trespasses." (Mark 11:25–26)

You ought rather to forgive and comfort him, lest perhaps such a one be swallowed up with too much sorrow. (2 Cor. 2:7)

Unconditional Love Is a Choice of the Will

Ultimately, unconditional love is a choice of your will. It is not a feeling as much as it is an act of *choosing* to respond to another person as God responds to that person. It is choosing to see another person through God's eyes and then relating to that person as God desires for you to relate to him or her. Read again these verses from the famous "love chapter" of the apostle Paul to the Corinthians, and, as you read, relate this passage of Scripture to your own family relationships:

Though I speak with the tongues of men and of angels, but have not love, I have become sounding brass or a clanging cymbal. And though I have the gift of prophecy, and under-stand all mysteries and all knowledge, and though I have all faith, so that I could remove mountains, but have not love, I am nothing. And though I bestow all my goods to feed the poor, and though I give my body to be burned, but have not love, it profits me nothing. Love suffers long and is kind; love does not envy; love does not parade itself, is not puffed up; does not behave rudely, does not seek its own, is not provoked, thinks no evil; does not rejoice in iniquity, but rejoices in the truth; bears all things, believes all things, hopes all things, endures all things. Love never fails. (1 Cor. 13:1–8)

- *What new insights do you have into this passage of Scripture and how this passage might relate to the protection of your family against evil?*

　　_____

　　_____

- *What new insights do you have about the nature of love to counteract evil forces that might attack your family?*

　　_____

　　_____

- *In what ways are you being challenged today?*

　　_____

　　_____

LESSON 5

KEEPING THE FAMILY FROM SPIRITUAL BONDAGE: PART 1

Perhaps the foremost challenge that we face as parents today is to *keep* our families out of spiritual bondage.

At the root of virtually every form of family dysfunction and disharmony, one finds a form of spiritual bondage. Name any problem that plagues the family today and if you trace that problem back to its root, you will find that the problem actually began in the spiritual realm. It had its seed of beginning in the heart of one person's rebellion against God.

Many forms and sources of bondage plague the family today. The vast majority of them do not involve demonic *possession,* but they all involve some form of demonic *oppression* and deceit.

In this lesson we will deal with three elements that can lead to spiritual "entrapment" by the enemy:

1. The lies of Satan.
2. Willful sin.
3. A careless lack of guarding our lives against evil.

The Lies of Satan Entrap Us

The lies of Satan serve as a trap or a snare. A multitude of lies, when accepted as truth by a person, serve as tiny threads that encircle the spirit—round and round and round—until the person is trapped, oppressed, restricted, "bound."

Most of the lies that Satan speaks to us are not giant "ropes." If they were, we'd recognize them immediately and reject them. Rather, the lies of Satan often seem to us to be innocent little "white lies," small errors against God's Word, getting off the path of God's way just a degree or two. These lies are like hundreds of tiny threads that, as a whole, bind us spiritually. And the fact is, if you wrap enough sewing thread around a person, you can entrap a person just as securely as if you wrapped a few heavy ropes around him.

Some families are in bondage because the father is an alcoholic, enslaved to a chemical that has the potential to destroy not only himself but his entire family. Somewhere along the line, this father bought into the lie, "One little drink won't hurt you." And then another lie: "A few drinks never hurt anybody, and they won't hurt you." And then another lie: "You are in control of your drinking, and as long as you are in control, you are all right." And then another lie and another until the man was in bondage, no longer in control of his drinking or his resulting negative behavior. He eventually entered a state of oppression that impacted his family and put his wife and children into a form of bondage as well.

The same pattern applies to any form of chemically induced bondage: the use of illegal drugs, overuse of prescription medications, and the abuse of inhalants and other lesser known chemicals.

Some families are in bondage to bitterness. Consider a mother, for example, who has a deep-seated bitterness toward her husband . . . or toward her own mother or father or to another person. She once bought a lie of Satan: "You have justification to be bitter and to harbor this anger and hatred in your heart." That lie led to another: "How you feel is your business alone. Your feelings don't impact your husband or your children." And the lies continued as the bitterness built. The result, however, is now a family in which both husband and children "tiptoe" around Mom because nobody is quite sure what will set her off or how her bitterness will be spewed out against them. Such a family is in bondage—not free in spirit, not honest in communication, not genuinely loving in an unconditional, generous way.

Some families are in bondage related to the use of pornography, an illicit sexual affair, or a spirit of greed that has wreaked havoc with the family finances. Jealousy, a sensual spirit, and a lust for material goods all can result in great personal and family bondage. Numerous forms of maladjustment and dysfunction result in bondage. All, however, began with a lie or a deceitful temptation of Satan.

When we are tempted by Satan and yield to that temptation, it is as if we open the door to our lives and our families and invite Satan to enter. If Satan can get one member of the family, and especially so the father, he has entry to the entire family. A man who willingly and repeatedly yields to Satan's temptation has no authority to keep Satan out of the lives of the rest of his family members.

- *Have you ever experienced a bondage in your family? Can you identify the initial lie or deceit of Satan that may have resulted in that bondage?*

  _____

  _____

What the Word Says

[Jesus said to those who lied about Him], "You are of your father the devil, and the desires of your father you want to do. He was a murderer from the beginning, and does not stand in the truth, because there is no truth in him. When he speaks a lie, he speaks from his own resources, for he is a liar and the father of it." (John 8:44)

What the Word Says to Me

_____

_____

_____

_____

_____

_____

_____

_____

_____

_____

So the great dragon was cast out,
that serpent of old, called the
Devil and Satan, who deceives the
whole world; he was cast to the
earth, and his angels were cast out
with him. (Rev. 12:9)

_____
_____
_____
_____
_____
_____

The LORD hates . . .
a false witness who speaks lies.
(Prov. 6:16, 19)

_____
_____
_____

Sin Puts Us in Bondage

A prevailing truth in God's Word is this: sin creates spiritual bondage. In fact, sin is the root source of bondage. Many other factors may contribute to or intensify bondage, but sin against God is the central and foremost factor that creates the spiritual bondage that, in turn, gives rise to both personal and family problems.

Can a person sin repeatedly and not experience bondage? No. A pattern of sin in a person's life will always result in bondage, which is also described in the Bible as enslavement or "dominion."

Romans 6:13–16 tells us,

> And do not present your members as instruments of unrighteousness to sin, but present yourselves to God as being alive from the dead, and your members as instruments of righteousness to God. For sin shall not have dominion over you, for you are not under law but under grace. What then? Shall we sin because we are not under law but under grace? Certainly not! Do you not know that to whom you present yourselves slaves to obey, you are that one's slaves whom you obey, whether of sin leading to death, or of obedience leading to righteousness?

A number of people have confessed to me down through the years that they _knew_ they were sinning from the outset of the sin that put their families into bondage, but they tried to convince themselves, "I'll stop this after a while. One of these days, I'll turn around and break loose of this." They felt they had power over sin.

The truth of God's Word is that the impulses a person obeys and the desires that a person acts upon have power over the person. They rule, dictate, and control.

In the case of alcohol, the person takes a drink. The drink desire increases. Eventually the drink takes the person.

In the case of anger and hatred, the person feels anger and hate. The anger and hatred build. Eventually the anger and hatred dictate what the person does, perceives, feels, thinks, and chooses to act upon.

Bondage begins when we sin against God. It becomes increasingly entrenched the longer we continue in the sin.

- *How does it feel to be in bondage?*

_____

_____

The Power of a Single Sin

Massive family problems as well as rather minor family problems can have as their source a single sinful act born of one family member's will. One person decides to do things his or her way, contrary to God's way. One person wants something, desires something, does something, or says something that is born of a rebellious or proud heart—in opposition to the Word of God and God's plan for the family.

I have counseled families in which the problem that threatened a long-standing marriage began with just one hurtful and unloving statement rooted in anger and bitterness. One act of infidelity. One "experimentation" with a chemical. One dishonest transaction. One lie. One turn of a cold shoulder toward a family member in need.

That one willful, sinful act may have prompted other family members to *react* in sinful and willful ways. The problem may have compounded until it was so complex that it was virtually unsolvable by the human mind. Nevertheless, in reality, the problem began simply: a single act of sin.

- *Can you identify a problem in your family, or a family you know, that began with a single act of rebellion against God's Word and God's plan for the family?*

_____

_____

The Bible is very clear on the fact that *all* sin has negative consequences. Ultimately, the consequence for an unredeemed sin nature is eternal death. On this earth, however, we also experience something of a "death" inside us when we sin. Sin causes a part of our inner conscience and soul to die—we might call it a loss of innocence, a callousness of conscience, a hardening of the heart. We experience an inner torment, which we sometimes are even hard-pressed to identify.

Within a family, sin on the part of one or more family members can cause trust to die, and ultimately it can kill a relationship.

Furthermore, when one member of the family enters into sin and that sin goes unrepented, the result is generally more sin. Sin becomes unchecked within the family, and Satan is allowed greater and greater influence until not only the initial sinner but the entire family is in bondage.

Never wink at sin in your life or the lives of your family members. Never say, "Oh, it was just a little lie, it was just a little dishonesty, it was just a little angry outburst." The best time to deal with sin is at its inception. Call sin for what it is—a deadly disease in both the individual's life and the life of your family. Teach your children to recognize sin and call it for what it is. Be quick to respond to sin by calling a person to repentance and to a change of behavior. Be quick to ask for God's forgiveness when you sin and to pray with your children to receive God's forgiveness when you know—and they know!—that they have sinned. The good news for each of us is that God is quick to forgive our sin when we come to Him with a humble and honest heart, admitting our sin and seeking His forgiveness.

One of the most important psalms that you should teach your children, and that you might consider reading often in your home, is Psalm 51, a portion of which is provided below:

Have mercy upon me, O God,
According to Your lovingkindness;
According to the multitude of Your tender mercies,
Blot out my transgressions.
Wash me thoroughly from my iniquity,
And cleanse me from my sin.

For I acknowledge my transgressions,
And my sin is always before me.
Against You, You only, have I sinned,
And done this evil in Your sight—
That You may be found just when You speak,
And blameless when You judge.
. . . .
Purge me with hyssop, and I shall be clean;
Wash me, and I shall be whiter than snow.
Make me hear joy and gladness,
That the bones You have broken may rejoice.
Hide Your face from my sins,
And blot out all my iniquities.

Create in me a clean heart, O God,
And renew a steadfast spirit within me. (Ps. 51:1–4, 7–10)

- *What new insights do you have into this passage of Scripture?*

  _____

  _____

What the Word Says

For the wages of sin is death, but
the gift of God is eternal life in
Christ Jesus our Lord. (Rom.
6:23)

Exhort one another daily, while it
is called "Today," lest any of you
be hardened through the deceit-
fulness of sin. (Heb. 3:13)

What the Word Says to Me

_____

_____

_____

_____

_____

_____

_____

_____

Giving Ready Access to Satan

At times Satan seems to enter our families through an unlocked door. On these occasions, he doesn't need to launch any major assault or even engage in persistent temptation. It is as if we provide ready access for uninvited entry.

How might this happen?

- By not training our children in the commandments of God.
- By not setting limits and boundaries.
- By not taking charge of our schedules and establishing our priorities so that God, His Word, and the church are of paramount importance to us as a family.
- By not choosing and then intentionally pursuing God's plan for authority and responsibility within the family.

The sin in this case is one of *omission*—of failing to do what is right before God. When we fail to establish good, we are open prey to evil. When we fail to set standards for righteousness, the lack of standards results in unrighteousness.

A person can be a "good person" in the eyes of the world, and in many cases, the eyes of other church members, and still leave the door unlocked to Satan.

At times, the unlocked door is related to things that we allow into our homes that we should not allow. Let me give you a couple of examples.

I once had a woman say to me, "I wish I could keep my fifteen-year-old son from reading a certain pornographic magazine." I said, "Don't blame your son. You have the authority to keep that magazine out of your home."

She seemed stunned. "I have the authority?" she said with a giant question mark in her voice.

"Yes," I said. "You have authority over your son as long as he is in your home and you are responsible for him legally, financially, socially, and morally. Those who have responsibility have authority."

She said, "But how can I keep him from bringing this magazine into our house?"

I said, "Don't let your son come through the door with it. Lock the door and then change the locks if you must. Let your son know that you will not allow certain items into your home. If he is going to live with you, he must abide by the rules you set for your home."

A Parent's Example Can Be an Unlocked Door

At other times, the parents unwittingly set an example that leaves an unlocked door in their children's lives. They want their children to "do what they say," unaware that their children are far more likely to "do what they do."

I've had parents complain to me that their children drink too much at college, but if you opened the door of the refrigerator in their homes, you'd find a six-pack of beer.

I've had parents moan that their young-adult children aren't going to church, but they do not see the relationship between their playing golf on Sunday mornings when those children were sixteen and eighteen years old and the fact that their children aren't attending church today.

I've had parents cry on my shoulder that their children run with a group of kids who watch all sorts of R-rated and X-rated movies and videos, but as I question them, I find that those same parents never took control of the television dial in their own home. In fact, those same parents watch R-rated and X-rated movies and videos themselves.

As parents, we must not *allow* certain things into our homes, and we must be very cautious in what we ourselves do. Our children will always test the limits and the boundaries we set. They will always copy our behavior. Any time we neglect to set proper boundaries or engage in improper behavior ourselves, we are leaving open a door that *should* have been locked against the enemy. We may not be overtly granting permission for our children to sin, but we certainly are making the access of Satan much easier into their lives. We must do our utmost to "lock the doors" spiritually if we hope to deter Satan's efforts in plundering our children.

The Primary Responsibility Belongs to Dad

Who is the person primarily responsible for making sure that the doors of the home are locked spiritually? The father.

In Matthew 12:29 Jesus said, "How can one enter a strong man's house and plunder his goods, unless he first binds the strong man? And then he will plunder his house."

The "strong man" in a family is the father. He is the one who has the ultimate responsibility for and authority over his family members.

The word *house* in this verse can refer to the family as well as to a physical structure. We find this usage in 1 Timothy 3:2, 4 where it says, "A bishop then must be blameless . . . one who rules his own house well, having his children in submission with all reverence." A man does not rule his physical house, but rather, those in it; he has authority over and responsibility for the members who reside in the house. In cases where the father is not in the home, the mother has responsibility for her "house"—her children. Part of that responsibility is to be an active member of a church in which the pastor and other strong Christian men can be authority figures and role models for her sons and daughters.

The word *goods* means vessels—containers of precious value. This word can refer to family members, the most precious of all treasures to a husband and father. Satan desires to "plunder" our spouses and our children.

It is very difficult for a wife and children to defend themselves against the onslaught of Satan if the father is weak spiritually or is willingly in rebellion against God. They are "open prey" to Satan's efforts. Satan will always hit the father first and the hardest because he knows that if he gets the dad, he gets the family.

In like manner, the father is the key to his family's salvation. In Acts 16 we read about a jailer who fell before Paul and Silas with fear and trembling, asking, "Sirs, what must I do to be saved?" They said to him, "Believe on the Lord Jesus Christ, and you will be saved, you and your household" (Acts 16:30–31).

When a man accepts Jesus as Savior and begins to follow Him as Lord, it is much easier for that man's wife and children to come to the Lord and to follow Him on a daily basis. In fact, the closer a father follows Christ, the closer his family will follow Christ.

This does not mean that the children of every saved man will automatically be saved, but the chances are much much greater—

in fact, the percentage is extremely high—that saved parents will raise children who will accept Christ for themselves.

- *In your experience, what role did your father have in setting the spiritual tone for the family? What were the results?*

_____

_____

What the Word Says

We must give the more earnest heed to the things we have heard, lest we drift away. . . . how shall we escape if we neglect so great a salvation? (Heb. 2:1, 3)

Do not neglect the gift that is in you, which was given to you by prophecy with the laying on of the hands of the eldership. Meditate on these things; give yourself entirely to them, that your progress may be evident to all. Take heed to yourself and to the doctrine. Continue in them, for in doing this you will save both yourself and those who hear you. (1 Tim. 4:14–16)

Whatever things are true . . . noble . . . just . . . pure . . . lovely . . . of good report, if there is any virtue and if there is anything praiseworthy—meditate on these things. The things which you learned and received and heard and saw in me, these do, and the God of peace will be with you. (Phil. 4:8–9)

What the Word Says to Me

_____

_____

_____

_____

_____

_____

_____

_____

_____

_____

_____

_____

_____

_____

_____

_____

_____

_____

_____

_____

_____

_____

_____

_____

- *In what ways are you feeling challenged to take positive action to keep your family from spiritual bondage?*

_____

_____

KEEPING THE FAMILY FROM SPIRITUAL BONDAGE: PART 2

How can a family avoid spiritual bondage? We might conclude from our previous lesson that we should:

1. Refuse to listen to the lies of the devil (and refuse to yield to his temptations).
2. Do no sin.
3. Give no entrance to sinful influence.

A family that takes those three steps will be spared a great deal of trauma and trouble!

James 4:7 gives us two further keys: "Submit to God. Resist the devil and he will flee from you."

Submit to God

Submission to God occurs when we face up to our own sinful nature and say to God, "I am a sinner in need of Your forgiveness.

Please forgive me and fill me with Your Holy Spirit so that I can truly change my life and live in a way that is pleasing to You." Submission is a total yielding of ourselves to God.

God desires for our submission to Him to be total—nothing held back. We are to give Him our talents, our timetables, our desires, our hopes, our possessions, our lives, our relationships, our resources, our work, our *all*.

Once we are in right relationship with God, we face a daily submission of our will. No person is capable of completely submitting all to Christ and then never having to submit again. Submission is ongoing. It requires a continual yielding of our will to His will for us. We must come to God every day and say, "Guide me, Holy Spirit. Lead me in the ways in which I should go. Cause me to say what I am to say, to make the decisions that are right before God, and to do the things I am to do."

What the Word Says	What the Word Says to Me
I beseech you therefore, brethren, by the mercies of God, that you present your bodies a living sacrifice, holy, acceptable to God, which is your reasonable service. And do not be conformed to this world, but be transformed by the renewing of your mind, that you may prove what is that good and acceptable and perfect will of God. (Rom. 12:1–2)	_____
And do not present your members as instruments of unrighteousness to sin, but present yourselves to God as being alive from the dead, and your members as instruments of righteousness to God. (Rom. 6:13)	_____
The LORD will guide you continually,	_____

And satisfy your soul in drought.   ------------------------------
(Isa. 58:11)   ------------------------------

- *Have you truly submitted your life to Christ Jesus—all that you are and all that you have?*

Submission to God's Commandments

One thing we can be certain about is this: the Holy Spirit will always lead us to live in full accordance with God's commandments. Nothing the Holy Spirit ever directs you to say or do will be contrary to the Bible.

God has a path for you to walk within. His commandments are His "limitations"—like hedges along that path. The commandments give us a clear direction about how we are to live as individuals and as families.

You are wise to remind yourselves frequently *as a family* of God's commandments, and as parents, to use them as the basis for setting limitations on your children. As you establish rules for your child, here are some principles to follow:

Make your instructions and rules clear. Be precise. Speak in a language your child understands. You may need to add when you tell your young child to "clean out the flower bed" that you mean for him to leave the soil! God has made His commandments very clear and direct in the Bible. They are readily understood. Make sure your family rules and instructions are equally clear.

Whenever possible, explain to your children why *you are giving certain limitations.* Have a reason for your family rules. God certainly has an ultimate plan and reason behind the commandments He has given us. They clearly are for our good. The rules you establish for your family should also be for good, not out of habit or from self-centered desire.

Establish consequences for disobeying family rules. God has told us very clearly that when we break His commandments, we will suffer consequences. Match your disciplinary measures to the disobedience.

Establish rewards for obeying family rules. Just as God has said in His Word that we are subject to chastisement when we disobey Him, so He has said that He is a "rewarder" to those who are faithful in obeying Him. Your children, too, need to be rewarded and praised for their good behavior. Rewards are far more motivating than threats of punishment.

What the Word Says

There are three that bear witness in heaven: the Father, the Word, and the Holy Spirit; and these three are one. (1 John 5:7)

Abhor what is evil. Cling to what is good. (Rom. 12:9)

Refuse the evil and choose the good. (Is. 7:16)

Be strong and very courageous, that you may observe to do according to all the law which Moses My servant commanded you; do not turn from it to the right hand or to the left, that you may prosper wherever you go. This Book of the Law shall not depart from your mouth, but you shall meditate in it day and night, that you may observe to do according to all that is written in it. For then you will make your way prosperous, and then you will have good success. (Josh. 1:7–8)

He who comes to God must believe that He is, and that He is a rewarder of those who diligently seek him. (Heb. 11:6)

What the Word Says to Me

Please, obey the voice of the LORD
which I speak to you. So it shall be
well with you, and your soul shall
live. (Jer. 38:20)

_____
_____
_____
_____

- *In what ways are you feeling challenged to lead your family into greater submission to God and His commandments?*

_____
_____

Resist the Devil

Resisting the devil is sometimes as simple as just saying no to his temptations. At other times, the assault of the devil is stronger against our lives, and we must put up an even greater defense against evil. How do we do that?

First, we must pray and ask God for help. None of us are a match for the devil in our own strength. But . . . the devil is never a match for *us and God.* The Lord with us is far greater than any force for evil.

Make daily prayer a habit in your family. Gather together in the morning as a family to "give your day to God." Ask for God's help, provision, and protection for the things that you are facing during the course of the day. Gather again as a family at night to thank God for being with you and ask Him to watch over you as you sleep.

Let your children hear you pray, and especially let them hear (or overhear) you pray for them very personally, by name. Build into your children an understanding that you *believe* in God and that you *trust* God to help you every day of your life.

Second, we must learn how to use the Word of God against the devil. Read again the way in which Jesus confronted and resisted Satan when he came to Jesus in the wilderness:

> Now when the tempter came to Him, he said, "If You are the Son of God, command that these stones become bread." But He answered and said, "It is written, 'Man shall not live by bread alone, but by every word that proceeds from the mouth of God.'" [Deut. 8:3]

Then the devil took Him up into the holy city, set Him on the pinnacle of the temple, and said to Him, "If You are the Son of God, throw Yourself down. For it is written: 'He shall give His angels charge over you,' and, 'In their hands they shall bear you up, lest you dash your foot against a stone.'"

Jesus said to him, "It is written again, 'You shall not tempt the LORD your God.'" [Deut. 6:16]

Again, the devil took Him up on an exceedingly high mountain, and showed Him all the kingdoms of the world and their glory. And he said to Him, "All these things I will give You if You will fall down and worship me.'"

Then Jesus said to him, "Away with you, Satan! For it is written, 'You shall worship the LORD your God, and Him only you shall serve.'" [Deut. 6:13] (Matt. 4:3–10)

• *What new insights do you have from this passage of Scripture?*

_____

_____

Three times Satan came to Jesus to tempt Him, and three times Jesus resisted the devil's temptation by using the Word of God. We are wise to do the same!

Of course, to use the Scriptures in resisting the devil we must *know* the Scriptures. Make reading God's Word a daily habit in your family. You might choose to read the Bible together as a family, or you might choose to establish a "quiet time" in which each family member reads the Word for himself. It is very helpful to some families for each person to be reading the same chapters of the Bible during "individual" daily devotions; mealtime conversations can then be focused in part on the insights into God's Word that each person gleaned.

John tells us that the temptations of Satan are focused on three areas: "the lust of the flesh, the lust of the eyes, and the pride of life" (1 John 2:16). You can count on the devil to come to you and your family and tempt you repeatedly to fulfill the lusts of your physical flesh, to fulfill your desire for more and more things, and to desire more and more status. Warn your children in advance that these temptations *will* come, and give your children the scriptural tools to counteract these temptations.

Help your child to memorize verses that speak of God's purity, the adequacy of God's provision (including satisfaction with and thanksgiving for God's material supply), and the humility of heart that God desires for us.

What the Word Says

Be sober, be vigilant; because your adversary the devil walks about like a roaring lion, seeking whom he may devour. Resist him, steadfast in the faith. (1 Peter 5:8–9)

Take the helmet of salvation, and the sword of the Spirit, which is the word of God; praying always with all prayer and supplication in the Spirit, being watchful to this end with all perseverance and supplication for all the saints. (Eph. 6:17–18)

For the word of God is living and powerful, and sharper than any two-edged sword, piercing even to the division of soul and spirit, and of joints and marrow, and is a discerner of the thoughts and intents of the heart. (Heb. 4:12)

My son, if you receive my words,
And treasure my commands within you,
So that you incline your ear to wisdom,
And apply your heart to

What the Word Says to Me

----

understanding;
Yes, if you cry out for discern-
ment,
And lift up your voice for under-
standing,
If you seek her as silver,
And search for her as for hidden
treasures;
Then you will understand the fear
of the LORD,
And find the knowledge of God.
For the LORD gives wisdom;
From His mouth come knowledge
and understanding;
He stores up sound wisdom for
the upright;
He is a shield to those who walk
uprightly;
He guards the paths of justice,
And preserves the way of His
saints.
Then you will understand righ-
teousness and justice,
Equity and every good path.
(Prov. 2:1–9)

- *Have you had an experience in which you resisted the devil through prayer and a quoting of God's Word? What happened?*

_____

_____

- *In what ways are you feeling challenged today to arm yourself and your family members with God's Word?*

_____

_____

LESSON 7

LAYING A FIRM FOUNDATION

We all know the old adage, "The best defense is a good offense." Proverbs 22:6 provides the good offense for protecting your family: "Train up a child in the way he should go, / And when he is old he will not depart from it."

Training involves two essentials:

1. A focus on teaching the "right" things to do.
2. Practice in doing the right things.

Teaching the Right Things

In the last lesson we focused on several right things to do in your family: submit your life to God and read and study the Word of God so you might submit to God's commandments and use the Scriptures in resisting the devil.

The greatest thing you can ever do for your child is to share the gospel with him or her. Make God's plan of salvation very clear to your child—that God sent His Son, Jesus, to die a sacrificial death on the cross so that your child might be freed of the penalty of death that is given to sin. When your child believes on Jesus Christ as Savior and receives God's forgiveness, your child is spiritually reborn into the kingdom of God. At that point, the Holy Spirit indwells your child to help your child live a life that is pleasing to God and that brings great blessings, now and into eternity.

A part of every parent's challenge is to prepare a child for full accountability to God. The parent's role is to guide a child to the point where he has a deep inner sense of personal responsibility for his behavior and choices and accountability to Almighty God for both his attitudes and actions. Because children are concrete thinkers, this sense of responsibility and accountability must first be required in the home: a child must know from infancy that he is accountable to his parents, who are responsible for him under God's authority. Increasingly, a child is to be held responsible for his own behavior and for being accountable directly to God. By the time a child reaches adulthood, he should feel completely responsible for his own life and fully accountable to God, who is the supreme authority over his life. This process is one of spiritual maturation with the parent as chief overseer and teacher.

In teaching your child accountability to God, you also are teaching the "chain of authority" under which we all live. Every person is subject to someone, and ultimately, we are all subject to God. Submission one to another is a repeated theme in the New Testament epistles. A child who does not learn to submit to parental authority is a child who will be rebellious against all authority, and in the end, will be rebellious against God's authority. Don't let that happen! Insist that your child obey you.

- *In what ways were you prepared in your early life to be accountable to God, responsible for your own behavior, and to trust God as the highest authority over your life?*

  _____

  _____

- *In what ways are you feeling challenged today in your parenting role?*

  _____

  _____

What the Word Says

We shall all stand before the judgment seat of Christ. . . . So then each of us shall give account of himself to God. (Rom. 14:10, 12)

For we must all appear before the judgment seat of Christ, that each one may receive the things done in the body, according to what he has done, whether good or bad. (2 Cor. 5:10)

Let every soul be subject to the governing authorities. For there is no authority except from God, and the authorities that exist are appointed by God. Therefore whoever resists the authority resists the ordinance of God, and those who resist will bring judgment on themselves. For rulers are not a terror to good works, but to evil. Do you want to be unafraid of the authority? Do what is good, and you will have praise from the same. For he is God's minister to you for good. But if you do evil, be afraid; for he does not bear the sword in vain; for he is God's minister, an avenger to execute wrath on him who practices evil. Therefore you must be subject, not only because of wrath but also for conscience' sake. (Rom. 13:1–5)

What the Word Says to Me

The Right Things

In addition to teaching a child how to accept Christ Jesus as Savior, how to mature into accountability for his life, and how to respect authority, there are a number of other things that are vitally important that you teach your child in order to protect him from evil. Among those "right" principles are these eight:

1. *The sovereignty of God.* The central concept of the Bible is that there is only *one God*, sovereign and almighty. He is our creator, our provider, our sustainer, our deliverer. He is King of kings and Lord of lords.

What the Word Says	What the Word Says to Me
Hear, O Israel: The LORD our God, the LORD is one! You shall love the LORD your God with all your heart, with all your soul, and with all your strength. (Deut. 6:4–5)	_____
And God spoke all these words, saying: "I am the LORD your God. . . . You shall have no other gods before Me." (Ex. 20:1–3)	_____

2. *Reliability of Scripture.* As you teach your child the Bible, do so with the perspective that the Bible is true and it can be trusted. Don't teach the Bible as a storybook, but rather, as truth on which your child can base his eternal future and all of life's decisions.

What the Word Says	What the Word Says to Me
All Scripture is given by inspiration of God, and is profitable for doctrine, for reproof, for correction, for instruction in righteousness, that the man of God may be complete, thoroughly equipped for every good work. (2 Tim. 3:16–17)	_____

I have not departed from Your
judgments,
For You Yourself have taught me.
How sweet are Your words to my
taste,
Sweeter than honey to my mouth!
Through Your precepts I get
understanding;
Therefore I hate every false way.
Your word is a lamp to my feet
And a light to my path.
(Ps.119:102–5)

3. *How to forgive others.* Teach your child the importance of forgiveness and also how to apologize to others, ask forgiveness of others, and make amends in righting wrongs.

What the Word Says	What the Word Says to Me
For You, Lord, are good, and ready to forgive, And abundant in mercy to all those who call upon You. (Ps. 86:5)	
[Jesus taught His disciples to pray]: "Forgive us our debts, As we forgive our debtors." (Matt. 6:12)	

4. *How to trust God in every circumstance.* A recent research study found that when teens are under stress, they turn to *music* as their first resort for comfort. Mom was number thirty-one on the list and Dad was number forty-eight. Counselors, teachers, and pastors were all tied at number fifty-four, which was at the bottom of the list! When tough times come, as they invariably do, your child needs to first trust God and, second, come to you as a parent for comfort and counsel. The way you teach trust to your child is to

be trustworthy. Keep your child's secrets, follow through on what you say you will do for and with your child, and be present for your child in experiences that require courage or fortitude (even without your child asking you to be present).

What the Word Says	What the Word Says to Me
In that day you shall not be shamed for any of your deeds In which you transgress against Me; For then I will take away from your midst Those who rejoice in your pride, And you shall no longer be haughty In My holy mountain. I will leave in your midst A meek and humble people, And they shall trust in the name of the LORD. (Zeph. 3:11–12)	_____ _____ _____ _____ _____ _____ _____ _____ _____ _____ _____ _____
It is better to trust in the LORD Than to put confidence in man. It is better to trust in the LORD Than to put confidence in princes. (Ps. 118:8–9)	_____ _____ _____ _____ _____
We trust in the living God, who is the Savior of all men, especially of those who believe. (1 Tim. 4:10)	_____ _____ _____

5. *God's law of sowing and reaping.* God's Word is very clear: what we sow, we reap; what we give, we receive. Teach your child to give generously. Reward your child for good behavior; chastise your child for bad behavior, always with the intent of correcting that behavior and never with the intent of wounding the spirit of your child. A part of your child's sowing needs to be giving to the church. Even a young child can give a tithe of his or her allowance. Put your

child into a position of receiving the blessings associated with the tithe (Mal. 3:10–11).

What the Word Says	What the Word Says to Me
Do not be deceived, God is not mocked; for whatever a man sows, that he will also reap. For he who sows to his flesh will of the flesh reap corruption, but he who sows to the Spirit will of the Spirit reap everlasting life. And let us not grow weary while doing good, for in due season we shall reap if we do not lose heart. (Gal. 6:7–9)	------------------------------- ------------------------------- ------------------------------- ------------------------------- ------------------------------- ------------------------------- ------------------------------- ------------------------------- -------------------------------
Give, and it will be given to you: good measure, pressed down, shaken together, and running over will be put into your bosom. For with the same measure that you use, it will be measured back to you. (Luke 6:38)	------------------------------- ------------------------------- ------------------------------- ------------------------------- ------------------------------- ------------------------------- -------------------------------
"Bring all the tithes into the storehouse, That there may be food in My house, And try Me now in this," Says the LORD of hosts, "If I will not open for you the windows of heaven And pour out for you such blessing That there will not be room enough to receive it. And I will rebuke the devourer for your sakes, So that he will not destroy the fruit of your ground,	------------------------------- ------------------------------- ------------------------------- ------------------------------- ------------------------------- ------------------------------- ------------------------------- ------------------------------- ------------------------------- ------------------------------- ------------------------------- ------------------------------- -------------------------------

Nor shall the vine fail to bear fruit for you in the field." (Mal. 3:10–11)

6. *How to find identity in Christ Jesus.* Teach your child that even as your child grows physically, intellectually, and emotionally, he is also to grow spiritually. Set the goal of Christ Jesus before your child—that he or she is to become more and more like Christ. It is in Christ that your child's inherent talents and gifts will find their full expression, for it is *as* your child ministers to others in the name of Jesus out of the abilities and talents he has been given by God that your child will truly experience satisfaction and fulfillment in life. Help your child discover his talents, develop them fully, and then *use* them in some form of ministry to others.

What the Word Says

Jesus increased in wisdom and stature, and in favor with God and men. (Luke 2:52)

He Himself gave some to be apostles, some prophets, some evangelists, and some pastors and teachers, for the equipping of the saints for the work of ministry, for the edifying of the body of Christ, till we all come to the unity of the faith and of the knowledge of the Son of God, to a perfect man, to the measure of the stature of the fullness of Christ; that we should no longer be children, tossed to and fro and carried about with every wind of doctrine, by the trickery of men, in the cunning craftiness of deceitful plotting, but, speaking the truth in love, may grow up in all things into

What the Word Says to Me

Him who is the head—Christ—
from whom the whole body,
joined and knit together by what
every joint supplies, according to
the effective working by which
every part does its share, causes
growth of the body for the edifying of itself in love. (Eph.
4:11–16)

7. *How to experience the work of the Holy Spirit.* The Holy Spirit
works within the heart of man to reveal to us the truth—in other
words, to prick our consciences of right and wrong. Teach your
child to be sensitive to the working of the Holy Spirit and to act
upon the impulses for good that the Holy Spirit prompts in him.
Teach your child that the character traits of God's own Spirit are
what God desires as the character traits of your child (Gal. 5:22–23).

What the Word Says

[Jesus comforted His disciples in
saying]: "But when the Helper
comes, whom I shall send to you
from the Father, the Spirit of
truth who proceeds from the
Father, He will testify of Me. . . . If
I depart, I will send Him to you.
And when He has come, He will
convict the world of sin, and of
righteousness, and of judgment."
(John 15:26 and 16:7–8)

But the fruit of the Spirit is love,
joy, peace, longsuffering, kindness, goodness, faithfulness,
gentleness, self-control. Against
such there is no law. . . . If we live
in the Spirit, let us also walk in the
Spirit. (Gal. 5:22–23, 25)

What the Word Says to Me

8. *The power of faith in Christ Jesus.* Teach your child that the most potent force within him is faith in Christ Jesus. Faith is to be exercised, to be used so that it will grow strong and become *great* faith. It is by faith that we are called to live as Christians (Rom. 1:17).

What the Word Says	What the Word Says to Me
For I am not ashamed of the gospel of Christ, for it is the power of God to salvation for everyone who believes, for the Jew first and also for the Greek. For in it the righteousness of God is revealed from faith to faith; as it is written, "The just shall live by faith." (Rom. 1:16–17)	_____
For we walk by faith, not by sight. (2 Cor. 5:7)	_____

- *In your life, recall ways in which you have learned these vital foundational lessons. What has been the resulting benefit to you?*

  _____

  _____

- *In what ways are you being challenged to lay a foundation of right spiritual principles in your family?*

  _____

  _____

The Nature of Training

The eight lessons described above are part of the *content* that we are to teach within our families. The *method* by which we are to teach, however, is *training*. Training is not the expression or the telling of principles alone, although it includes the telling of principles. Training is rooted in doing, and especially in repetitive doing.

You will not teach your child to give and receive, for example, by telling your child to give. Your child will learn this lesson as he actually gives something that is valuable to him—and not only once, but repeatedly.

You will not teach your child the sovereignty of God by taking your child to church once so that your child might hear the Word of God preached or participate in praise and worship of God. Your child will learn this lesson as he or she attends church week in and week out, year in and year out, and especially as your child begins to take an active part in Bible study, praise, and various acts of worship and ministry.

You will not teach your child the fruit of the Spirit by telling your child what that fruit is, but, rather, by instilling in your child the behaviors that are associated with love, joy, peace, long-suffering, kindness, goodness, faithfulness, gentleness, and self-control. You will train your child in these character traits by *insisting* as an authority over your child that your child display patience, manifest goodness, be faithful in doing what he says he will do, and in exercising self-control.

Rewards and chastisements are always a part of the training process. When a child errs in behavior, he should be chastised. When a child succeeds in behavior, he should be rewarded.

As your child grows and matures, lead your child to an understanding of what it means to "self-train," which is to set limits for oneself. Allow your child to set standards and parameters for his life. For example, discuss with your child an appropriate curfew time; let your child be a part of the decision-making process. As you decide together a good curfew time, also determine in conversation with your child what the rewards and chastisements might be in relation to keeping curfew.

Give your child ample room to learn to trust God for himself—to pray and believe for things that are important to him, to trust God for outcomes and consequences, to give a witness of his faith, to see what God will do in the lives of others, and to engage in a form of ministry that is appropriate for your child's age and talents.

We are to be *doers* of the Word. The epistle of James makes it very clear that our faith must be an active faith—that while works do not bring about our salvation, they are vitally important to securing within us a full identity as God's child.

The child who is untrained in Christian disciplines and principles is a child who grows up thinking that sin has no penalty and that no authority can or should be exerted over him. Such a child manifests rebellion against parents and rebellion against God. Sadly, the child who violates spiritual principles discovers that happiness and joy are highly elusive, since neither inner peace nor joy can coexist with rebellion. The rebellious child is insecure because the foundation on which he stands is shifting continually. Such a child not only leads a destructive life, but his own life is destroyed, perhaps for all eternity.

- *Recall an instance in your life in which you were* trained *to do what was right. What was the result?*

_____

_____

- *How does it feel to develop mastery of a skill through training?*

_____

_____

What the Word Says

Faith by itself, if it does not have works, is dead. But someone will say, "You have faith, and I have works." Show me your faith without your works, and I will show you my faith by my works. You believe that there is one God. You do well. Even the demons believe—and tremble! But do you want to know, O foolish man, that faith without works is dead? Was not Abraham our father justified

What the Word Says to Me

_____

_____

_____

_____

_____

_____

_____

_____

_____

_____

_____

by works when he offered Isaac his son on the altar? Do you see that faith was working together with his works, and by works faith was made perfect? And the Scripture was fulfilled which says, "Abraham believed God, and it was accounted to him for righteousness." And he was called the friend of God. You see then that a man is justified by works, and not by faith only. (James 2:17–24)

As you therefore have received Christ Jesus the Lord, so walk in Him, rooted and built up in Him and established in the faith, as you have been taught, abounding in it with thanksgiving. (Col. 2:6–7)

- *In what ways are you being challenged to further train your child in right behaviors?*

By the Grace of God

While there is no substitute for doing the "good" things that protect us from the devil and from evil in the world, we also must acknowledge that there is no "sure formula" for keeping a child or an entire family from all harm or evil spiritual attack. We each are brought to the position of saying, "It is only by the grace of God."

What we can say with assurance is that God is in control. He is sovereign—completely and totally omnipotent, omniscient, omnipresent, loving, and just. Jesus Christ is victor over Satan.

In any negative situation or circumstance, we can have the full confidence of these three truths:

1. *God knows what we are going through.* He may not have

caused the negative situation in which we find ourselves, but He certainly knows about the situation, and He has allowed it to happen for a *good* purpose that we may not see or understand at this time.

2. *God is with us in the circumstance we are facing.* He never leaves us nor forsakes us (Heb. 13:5). We can trust Him to deliver us from evil, to lead us into right decisions and right actions, and to help us face and overcome the troubles that seem to overwhelm us. He will help us deal with any pain, blame, or shame that we experience, and He *will* heal us and make us whole as we put our faith in Him.

3. *God's purposes* will *be brought to pass.* God's plan will be accomplished. He is both the author and the *finisher* of our faith (Heb. 12:2). His methods may elude our understanding, but His purposes are sure—He will accomplish the full redemption and refinement of His chosen and beloved children.

What the Word Says	What the Word Says to Me
[Jesus said], "I am with you always, even to the end of the age." (Matt. 28:20)	_____ _____ _____
Looking unto Jesus, the author and finisher of our faith, who for the joy that was set before Him endured the cross, despising the shame, and has sat down at the right hand of the throne of God. (Heb. 12:2)	_____ _____ _____ _____ _____ _____ _____

- *In what ways are you feeling challenged today to lay a firmer foundation for your family?*

_____

_____

LESSON 8

PULLING DOWN STRONGHOLDS

A spiritual stronghold is any area of resistance against the working of the Holy Spirit in a person's life. The apostle Paul addressed the issue of spiritual strongholds in writing to the Corinthians:

> For though we walk in the flesh, we do not war according to the flesh. For the weapons of our warfare are not carnal but mighty in God for pulling down strongholds, casting down arguments and every high thing that exalts itself against the knowledge of God, bringing every thought into captivity to the obedience of Christ. (2 Cor. 10:3–5)

Note specifically that a stronghold is rooted in an "argument" against God—a mind-set, attitude, or thought that is contrary to the will of God—and in "every high thing that exalts itself against the knowledge of God," which is an attitude of pride that says, in effect, "I don't need God, and I don't need to live according to God's plan, purposes, and commandments."

Every stronghold begins in the attitude realm; it begins in the mind and heart. The more a person argues against God and sets his pride in opposition to God, the stronger the "stronghold" becomes. Another way of thinking of a stronghold is to say that a negative, proud attitude toward God exerts a "strong hold" on a person. The person who is suffering from a spiritual stronghold is a person who is stubborn, hard-hearted, stiff-necked, and in all ways rebellious toward God.

A spiritual stronghold in the life of a family member can wreak havoc on family peace and harmony. A rebel in the midst of a family causes untold grief.

The good news offered by the apostle Paul is this: we *can* pull down these strongholds.

Being Alert to Strongholds

Every person has an area of human weakness, or a propensity to sin in a certain way. As a parent, you are wise to identify that area of weakness as quickly as possible in your child's life. In some children, it may be anger. In others, dishonesty or lying. No two children in a family are likely to be born with the same "bent" toward evil. You must deal with each child individually.

Very often, the propensity for a child to sin in a particular way is a reflection of a parent's propensity to sin. Even as you look at your child's life, be aware that your child may be mirroring *your* life. It is not enough to be honest about your child's tendency to sin; we each must have the courage to be honest about our own tendency to sin and deal with it by asking God's forgiveness and help.

How can you identify an area of spiritual weakness in your child? By studying and observing your child. Take time with your child. Listen intently to your child. Look for patterns of behavior over time. Part of your role as a parent is to see your child in the context of weeks, months, and years; you are the foremost person responsible for spotting long-standing "trends" in your child's behavior—physically, mentally, emotionally, and spiritually.

- *Have you identified the areas of spiritual weakness (prideful attitudes and justifying arguments) in your own life?*

_____

_____

- *Have you identified spiritual strongholds in the lives of your family members?*

_____

_____

Help Create a New Pattern

Once you have identified areas of spiritual weakness, sin, or pride, help your child to create a new pattern of thinking and acting. You can also help your spouse, and receive help from a spouse, in combating spiritual strongholds.

Talk to your child (or spouse) about the strongholds you perceive to exist. Do not do this in a judgmental or condemning manner, but, rather, in an objective and loving way. Let your child know that you see a trend in his or her life, but that you love your child and desire to help your child overcome that area of weakness. Map out a strategy together for how you will attempt to deal with this stronghold.

Guard your child in areas of spiritual weakness. This doesn't mean, of course, that you need to tiptoe around your child or attempt to isolate your child from all normal experiences, but, rather, that you guard what you allow in your home and who you allow your child to be with (such as a playmate, friend, or teammate). Keep your child from others who have the same area of spiritual weakness or pride in their lives. (Do the same for your spouse.)

Build up your child by praising and rewarding behaviors that show your child is attempting to do what is godly. If your child has a tendency to lie, for example, you will want to reward your child for truth-telling. If your child has a tendency to display outbursts of anger, praise and reward your child for times when he displays kindness. If your child seems to have a "short fuse," praise and reward your child for times in which your child shows patience. (Let your spouse know that you appreciate your spouse's efforts to break a stronghold pattern.)

Break the cycle that builds a stronghold. Strongholds become established when the mind tells the will to engage in a behavior and the person's emotions declare the actual behavior to be good, pleasurable, or desirable. Because the end result is "feeling good," the mind will be much more prone to tell the will to engage in that behavior again. And so the cycle goes. For example, if a child has the idea to steal a bit of candy from the store, and then he steals that piece of candy, he is likely to feel a certain degree of satisfaction and pleasure at having "gotten away with" his sin, plus he has the treat of the candy itself. A certain "high" will be registered in his mind, and he very likely will set his mind about the task of deciding what he might steal next. If that next theft is successful, it also will bring a "high"—in fact, probably a little "higher high." And so the cycle goes until the child is devising ways to steal more and bigger things. A stronghold has been established.

What breaks the stronghold? Making certain that the sin is punished and that there is no pleasure associated with it!

Throughout the Bible, we have numerous examples of God moving among His people in a very active way to break the spiritual strongholds that were developing in them. It is a humble spirit (opposite of pride) and a yielding heart that God desires. If you do not help your children acquire humility and a desire to "agree" with God, your child will face those lessons in an increasingly strong manner from others and, ultimately, from God. Spare your child the pain associated with being hard-hearted or stiff-necked.

As you read the passages below, ask yourself, "How might this apply to my family?"

What the Word Says	What the Word Says to Me
Can two walk together, unless they are agreed? (Amos 3:3)	------------------------------- -------------------------------
Circumcise the foreskin of your heart, and be stiff-necked no longer. For the LORD your God is God of gods and Lord of lords, the great God, mighty and awesome, who shows no partiality nor takes a bribe. He administers justice. . . . You shall	------------------------------- ------------------------------- ------------------------------- ------------------------------- ------------------------------- ------------------------------- ------------------------------- -------------------------------

fear the LORD your God; you shall
serve Him, and to Him you shall
hold fast. (Deut. 10:16–18, 20)

But if you do not obey Me, and
do not observe all these commandments . . . I will punish you
seven times more for your sins. I
will break the pride of your power.
(Lev. 26:14, 18–19)

- *In what ways are you feeling challenged to correct the behavior
of your child or children?*

Sins of "Attitude"

Keep in mind always that the attitude of your child is just as
important as your child's behavior. In the great majority of cases,
a negative attitude is a strong indicator of future bad behavior.

Negative attitudes are often displayed in behaviors such as pout-
ing, sulking, scowling, deeply sighing, and slamming doors. A child
with a bad attitude very likely seeks to be "left alone" or to be
allowed to throw a "silent tantrum." Such attitudes are the toehold
that lead to a spiritual stronghold. As a parent, you are wise to chastise and correct your child's attitudes as much as you do your child's
deeds. If you do not, you can count on those attitudes eventually
manifesting as behaviors that generally are highly negative and often
are explosive.

Reward your child's good attitudes. Praise your child for an attitude that is positive, kind, generous, loving, or good. Let your child
know that you value and appreciate such attitudes.

Attitudes are rooted in emotions as much as they are ideas. Your
child will absorb the "feelings" of your family life as much as he
will absorb anything you say or do. Guard your own attitude closely.
Your child will pick up on your attitude and mirror it back to you!

Many of us pass on the feelings and attitudes we acquired as a child without questioning them. We simply do as parents what we had done to us as children. Very often the feelings and attitudes that we have acquired are not godly and have no place in a Christian home. Break the cycle! Be aware of your own responses. Think back to the feelings you had as a child. Ask yourself, "Are these wise feelings to give to my own children?"

What the Word Says

If My people who are called by My name will humble themselves, and pray and seek My face, and turn from their wicked ways, then I will hear from heaven, and will forgive their sin and heal their land. (2 Chron. 7:14)

[Jesus said], "Blessed are the poor in spirit, For theirs is the kingdom of heaven." (Matt. 5:3)

And His mercy is on those who fear Him From generation to generation. He has shown strength with His arm; He has scattered the proud in the imagination of their hearts. He has put down the mighty from their thrones, And exalted the lowly. (Luke 1:50–52)

Humble yourselves under the mighty hand of God, that He may exalt you in due time. (1 Peter 5:6)

What the Word Says to Me

The Sin of Pride

The sin of pride, which is the root of every spiritual stronghold, is a sin common to all mankind. It is not easily confronted because we often are too proud to admit that we have pride! Pride is also not a sin that is easily eradicated for it goes to the core of our very nature and what we hold to be true about ourselves and about our relationship with God. As long as we think that we can do it on our own in any area of our lives, we are guilty of pride.

Pride leads to

- self-justification for sin,
- excuses for bad behavior,
- demanding of one's own way, and
- less regard for others.

Jesus must become our role model for humility and meekness if we are to overcome pride. The Holy Spirit must become our constant source of help if we are to both recognize and take a stand against pride in our lives.

In your family, do not allow your child to "justify" bad behavior by saying that "everybody is doing it" or "it wasn't all that bad." Accept no excuses for bad behavior.

In your family, refuse to allow a child to *demand* his own way by means of a temper tantrum, whining, or manipulation.

In your family, insist that each family member show respect and deference to other family members. Don't let a child set your family schedule, dominate a conversation, or destroy family gatherings through rudeness, anger, or inconsiderate behavior.

Set a tone for humility in your home.

Jesus is our example in this. As you read the two passages of Scripture below, consider what it means to be a humble person in your own family.

> Let this mind be in you which was also in Christ Jesus, who, being in the form of God, did not consider it robbery to be equal with God, but made Himself of no reputation, taking the form of a bondservant, and coming in the likeness

of men. And being found in appearance as a man, He humbled Himself and became obedient to the point of death, even the death of the cross. (Phil. 2:5–8)

[Jesus said], "Learn from Me, for I am gentle and lowly in heart, and you will find rest for your souls." (Matt. 11:29)

- *What new insights do you have into these two passages of Scripture?*

_____

_____

What the Word Says	What the Word Says to Me
Pride goes before destruction, And a haughty spirit before a fall. (Prov. 16:18)	
The LORD lifts up the humble; He casts the wicked down to the ground. (Ps. 147:6)	
All of you be submissive to one another, and be clothed with humility, for "God resists the proud, But gives grace to the humble." (1 Peter 5:5)	
Let nothing be done through selfish ambition or conceit, but in lowliness of mind let each esteem others better than himself. Let each of you look out not only for his own interests, but also for the interests of others. (Phil. 2:3–4)	

Ask the Lord to reveal to you any strongholds that are taking shape in your life or in the life of your family members. And then ask Him to help you to deal with those strongholds. Ask Him to reveal to you *how* you should respond, *when* you should respond, and to give you the *courage* to respond. Earlier is better than later when it comes to dealing with areas of spiritual weakness, pride, and strongholds of the mind and heart.

Keep in mind always that spiritual strongholds are not only the work of the devil in our lives, but they are the means by which the devil causes us to work on his behalf! If we truly are to protect our families from evil, then we must stop evil the instant it strikes our minds and hearts. We must truly bring "every thought into captivity to the obedience of Christ" (2 Cor. 10:5).

- *What new insights do you have into the cause and nature of spiritual strongholds?*

  _____

  _____

- *In what ways are you feeling challenged today to protect your family by pulling down spiritual strongholds?*

  _____

  _____

LESSON 9

BINDING SATAN

The only true and lasting means of deliverance from bondage comes through the power of Jesus Christ. There are many fine forms of "help" for those who are in bondage, but none of them are as effective or long-lasting as spiritual deliverance. The reason for this is simple: all bondage has its root in sin and in the spiritual condition of man. Unless the bondage is broken in the spiritual realm, remnants of the bondage will remain.

More than Confession of Sin?

Many people find themselves so much into the bondage of Satan's lies and deceit that a simple confession of sin is not enough. They may receive God's forgiveness, but they still feel enslaved by a pattern of behavior that has become a strong habit in their lives, such as the habit of drinking, the habit of thinking ill of others, the habit of overspending, or the habit of seeing every person as an enemy.

Confession of sin and God's forgiveness bring release from sin's consequences in the person's relationship with God, but it does not always bring release from sin's consequences in the person's daily habitual behavior, environment, or circumstances.

- *Cite an instance in which you know that you or another person has been forgiven of sin but the consequences associated with past sin still linger.*

_____

_____

Jesus Came to Set Us Free

Isaiah foretold this about Jesus' purpose and ministry on this earth:

> The Spirit of the Lord GOD is upon Me,
> Because the LORD has anointed Me
> To preach good tidings to the poor;
> He has sent Me to heal the brokenhearted,
> To proclaim liberty to the captives,
> And the opening of the prison to those who are bound;
> To proclaim the acceptable year of the LORD,
> And the day of vengeance of our God;
> To comfort all who mourn,
> To console those who mourn in Zion,
> To give them beauty for ashes,
> The oil of joy for mourning,
> The garment of praise for the spirit of heaviness;
> That they may be called trees of righteousness,
> The planting of the LORD, that He may be glorified. (Isa.
> 61:1–3)

Jesus boldly declared that this prophecy was fulfilled in His life, and those who witnessed His ministry knew it to be true (Luke 4:16–21). As believers in Christ Jesus, we are called to carry on His ministry on this earth. The mandate given to Jesus is our mandate. Jesus said that through the power of the Holy Spirit, we would do even "greater works" than those manifested by Him, perhaps not in "quality" of work, but certainly in quantity and application. He said, "He who believes in Me, the works that I do he will do also; and greater works than these he will do, because I go to My Father. And whatever you ask in My name, that I will do, that the Father may be glorified in the Son. If you ask anything in My name, I will do it" (John 14:12–14).

Jesus once sent out His disciples to engage in active ministry in His name. He sent them two by two, and He told them to go into a city and remain with one family that would give hospitality to them, and to proclaim the good news, that the presence, power, and peace of God were manifest in Jesus Christ. We are to do the same—beginning in our own families. We are to proclaim the good news that Jesus has come, He is present with us now, and He *will* defeat Satan at every turn.

Jesus came *actively* to counteract the work of Satan just as His disciples did! And we are to start that work in our own families.

• *In what ways have you been "set free" by Jesus Christ?*

_____

_____

What the Word Says	What the Word Says to Me
[Jesus said], "The thief does not come except to steal, and to kill, and to destroy. I have come that they may have life, and that they may have it more abundantly." (John 10:10)	_____ _____ _____ _____ _____ _____
For this purpose the Son of God was manifested, that He might destroy the works of the devil. (1 John 3:8)	_____ _____ _____ _____
The Lord appointed seventy others also, and sent them two by two before His face into every city and place where He Himself was about to go. Then He said to them, "The harvest truly is great, but the laborers are few; therefore pray the Lord of the harvest to send out laborers into His harvest. . . . And heal the sick there, and say to them, 'The kingdom of God has come near to you.' . . . . He who hears you hears Me, he	_____ _____ _____ _____ _____ _____ _____ _____ _____ _____ _____

who rejects you rejects Me, and he
who rejects Me rejects Him who
sent me." Then the seventy
returned with joy, saying, "Lord,
even the demons are subject to us
in Your name." And He said to
them, "I saw Satan fall like light-
ning from heaven. Behold, I give
you the authority to trample on
serpents and scorpions, and over
all the power of the enemy, and
nothing shall by any means hurt
you. Nevertheless do not rejoice
in this, that the spirits are subject
to you, but rather rejoice because
your names are written in
heaven." (Luke 10:1–2, 9, 16–20)

- *How do you feel about the fact that Jesus has called you to carry on His work?*

- *In what ways do you feel challenged to engage in the active ministry of Jesus within your own family?*

A Threefold Purpose

Note specifically the threefold purpose in our binding Satan in our families:

1. Release
2. Restoration
3. Restriction

Release

We are to "proclaim liberty to the captives, / And the opening of the prison to those who are bound" (Isa. 61:1). True freedom is only found in Christ Jesus. As we read in John 8:36, "If the Son makes you free, you shall be free indeed." We are to proclaim the gospel boldly and without hesitation. Satan cannot operate in the presence of the gospel. Revelation 12:11 assures us that we can overcome Satan by the "word of [our] testimony," which is a testimony about the power of Jesus Christ and the salvation that He purchased for us on the cross.

Restoration

Jesus' ministry is a constant example of restoring those who had were trapped by Satan—for example, those who were trapped by sickness, troubles, depression, or demonic snares. Jesus came to restore the lost to the Father.

In Luke we read about Jesus casting a legion of demons from a man in Gadera. This man was completely delivered. He had once lived among the tombs and the hogs, but after Jesus delivered him, he was found "sitting at the feet of Jesus, clothed and in his right mind" (Luke 8:35). The man begged Jesus that he might go back with Him to the other side of the Sea of Galilee, but Jesus said, "Return to your own house, and tell what great things God has done for you" (v. 39). Jesus *restored* this man to his right mind, to a right relationship with God, and to his family. When we bind Satan, we can expect the same results!

I believe there are many marriages that might be restored and many children who might return home to a right relationship with their parents if they could only return to parents who are truly "set free" from sin, operating in a right mind and with a right heart.

What the Word Says	What the Word Says to Me
[Jesus said], "Most assuredly, I say to you, whoever commits sin is a slave of sin. And a slave does not abide in the house forever, but a son abides forever. Therefore if the Son makes you free, you shall be free indeed." (John 8:34–36)	_____ _____ _____ _____ _____ _____ _____

[Jesus said], "The Spirit of the
LORD is upon Me,
Because He has anointed Me
To preach the gospel to the poor;
He has sent Me to heal the
brokenhearted,
To proclaim liberty to the captives
And recovery of sight to the blind,
To set at liberty those who are
oppressed;
To proclaim the acceptable year of
the LORD." (Luke 4:18–19)

Restriction

Jesus desires that we ask Him to restrict the power of Satan on the earth. God has given us a free will to choose God's way or the devil's way. We must voluntarily ask God, through Jesus Christ, to keep the devil from exercising influence on our lives and the lives of those for whom we are responsible.

God certainly *can* exert authority and control over anything and over all things as He wills. But God has given us choice. He wants us to *choose* to ask Him to restrict the activity of the devil against us—to move in a mighty way against the power of the enemy. This is what we call "binding" Satan spiritually.

In reality, we are not the ones who do the actual binding. Jesus is the One who does the binding. He is the One who has won the definitive victory over Satan and who is stronger than Satan on all accounts. Satan is stronger than any one human being, but he is never stronger than a human being who is filled with the Holy Spirit. The power of the Holy Spirit active and working *within us* is always a more potent force than the working of Satan *around us*. As 1 John 4:4 says, "He who is in you [the Holy Spirit] is greater than he [the devil] who is in the world."

What the Word Says

[Jesus said], "All authority has been given to Me in heaven and on earth." (Matt. 28:18)

What the Word Says to Me

Then they were all amazed, so
that they questioned among themselves, saying, "What is this? What
new doctrine is this? For with
authority He commands even the
unclean spirits, and they obey
Him." (Mark 1:27)

Our Binding "Weapons"

Jesus has given us three "weapons" by which we are to bind Satan:
the Word, the Blood, and the name of Jesus.

The Word

In Matthew 13:18–24, Jesus told a parable about a sower who
sowed seed with four different results:

> Therefore hear the parable of the sower: When anyone hears
> the word of the kingdom, and does not understand it, then
> the wicked one comes and snatches away what was sown in
> his heart. This is he who received seed by the wayside. (vv.
> 18–19)

Jesus is saying that the first bad thing that can happen to seed is
that it fails to germinate and take root—it falls onto the soil of those
who are ignorant of spiritual things. In 2 Corinthians 4:3–4, Paul
wrote, "If our gospel is veiled, it is veiled to those who are perish-
ing, whose minds the god of this age has blinded, who do not believe,
lest the light of the gospel of the glory of Christ, who is the image
of God, should shine on them."

Our first prayer must always be that Satan will be restricted and
will not be able to exercise his "snatching power" over the Word of
God being preached or taught. We must pray that Satan will be
prohibited from blinding the eyes or deafening the ears of those
who are in the presence of the preaching of the gospel.

What the Word Says

That the God of our Lord Jesus
Christ, the Father of glory, may

What the Word Says to Me

give to you the spirit of wisdom
and revelation in the knowledge of
Him, the eyes of your understanding being enlightened; that you
may know what is the hope of His
calling, what are the riches of the
glory of His inheritance in the
saints, and what is the exceeding
greatness of His power toward us
who believe. (Eph. 1:17–19)

He who has ears to hear, let him
hear! (Matt. 11:15; 13:9, 43)

The Blood

Satan cannot cross the "blood line" that has been placed around
those who accept Jesus Christ as their Savior and who truly believe
in the sacrificial death of Jesus on the cross—a death in which His
blood was shed for our sakes. We bind Satan by declaring to him
that we have been purchased by the shed blood of Christ Jesus. In
so doing, we are declaring that we are the "property" of God, not
the property of the devil. God has jurisdiction and power over our
lives, not Satan.

What the Word Says

[Jesus said to His disciples at the
Last Supper]: "This is My blood
of the new covenant, which is
shed for many for the remission of
sins." (Matt. 26:28)

Without shedding of blood there
is no remission. . . . so Christ was
offered once to bear the sins of
many. (Heb. 9:22, 28)

If we walk in the light as He is in
the light, we have fellowship with
one another, and the blood of

What the Word Says to Me

Jesus Christ His Son cleanses us
from all sin. (1 John 1:7)

The Name of Jesus

Any time we confront Satan, we must do so in the name of the
Lord Jesus Christ. It is in His name that we have authority over
evil. After Peter and John had spoken to a lame man in the name
of Jesus, the man was healed. All who saw the man standing, walk-
ing, leaping, and praising God were amazed, and the religious
officials became so angry that they imprisoned Peter and John.

The next day the authorities gathered to interrogate Peter and
John, and the Bible tells us, "Then Peter, filled with the Holy Spirit,
said to them, 'Rulers of the people and elders of Israel: If we this
day are judged for a good deed done to a helpless man, by what
means he has been made well, let it be known to you all, and to all
the people of Israel, that by the name of Jesus Christ of Nazareth,
whom you crucified, whom God raised from the dead, by Him this
man stands here before you whole'" (Acts 4:8–10).

There is great power in the name of Jesus! He has given us His
name to use in bringing healing and deliverance to those who are
oppressed, discouraged, and "sick" or "injured" in any area of their
lives!

What the Word Says

Therefore God also has highly
exalted Him and given Him the
name which is above every name,
that at the name of Jesus every
knee should bow, of those in
heaven, and of those on earth, and
of those under the earth, and that
every tongue should confess that
Jesus Christ is Lord, to the glory
of God the Father. (Phil. 2:9–11)

[Jesus said], "Whatever you ask in
My name, that I will do, that the

What the Word Says to Me

Father may be glorified in the
Son. If you ask anything in My
name, I will do it." (John
14:13–14)

Peter said, "Silver and gold I do
not have, but what I do have I give
you: In the name of Jesus Christ
of Nazareth, rise up and walk."
(Acts 3:6)

A Verbal Declaration

Note that each of the "weapons" Jesus has given to us for the binding of Satan are weapons that we exercise in the spirit realm *by our spoken words.* We are called to speak the name of Jesus, to speak about the blood of Christ, to speak the Word of God as we give our own personal word of testimony. We do not bind Satan by just thinking good thoughts or having the right attitude. Our faith is certainly at the foundation of our battle against Satan, but repeatedly we are told that our faith must be verbalized—it must be spoken aloud.

It is in our speaking the name of Jesus, the blood of Jesus, the Word of Jesus that we make the presence and power of Jesus real, ready, and available in any situation or circumstance. To desire, wish, hope, or believe that Jesus will deliver us from Satan is not enough. We must declare it to be so!

- *In what ways are you feeling challenged today to bind Satan's influence in your life or in the life of a family member?*

LESSON 10

Praying for and with Your Family

Perhaps the most important thing that you can do to protect your family from evil is to intercede in prayer daily for your family. We have a great example of this in a Bible person whom many people do not readily associate with intercessory prayer: Job.

The book of Job begins by telling us that Job was a man who was "blameless and upright, and one who feared God and shunned evil" (1:1). Job had seven sons and three daughters. We read in Job 1:5 that Job rose "early in the morning" to "offer burnt offerings according to the number of them all. For Job said, 'It may be that my sons have sinned and cursed God in their hearts.' Thus Job did regularly."

Even though Job's children were grown and lived in their own homes, Job continued to make sacrifices for his children every morning. In doing this, he was calling out to God on their behalf, requesting God's mercy on their lives. His prayer life for his family was a part of his very character; it was his nature to pray as a blameless and upright man who feared God and shunned evil.

We are called to follow in Job's example today. We are to live blameless and upright lives before our children and also to pray for our children daily, no matter how old they are or what circumstances they are in.

• *In your life, do you have people who pray for you daily? How do you feel when you know that someone is praying for you daily?*

_____

_____

A Hedge of Protection

God uses our prayers for others to establish a hedge of protection around them. This was Satan's lament when he sought to bring accusation against Job and to attack his life. He said, "Does Job fear God for nothing? Have You not made a hedge around him, around his household, and around all that he has on every side?" (Job 1:9–10). Job's life and his practice of intercession on behalf of his family were certainly major factors in God's creating a hedge of protection that Satan could not penetrate.

A "hedge" in Bible times was not a little row of bushes or shrubbery that might grow in a yard or garden. It was considered to be a high wall or a fortresslike structure. Anything that was "hedged in" was fully protected from attack.

The Bible tells us God's hedge around us is generally established in one of two ways:

1. Through angels
2. Through righteous people

These are the foremost "methods" God uses to provide protection for us.

Hedge of Angels

In Psalm 34:7 we read, "The angel of the LORD encamps all around those who fear Him, / And delivers them."

Elisha was a man who experienced an angelic hedge of angels. In 2 Kings 6 we read how the king of Syria was greatly troubled by Elisha, who kept telling the Israelite army his every move. He sought to kill Elisha. With that intent, the Syrian king discovered that Elisha was residing in Dothan. The Bible says that the king of Syria

> sent horses and chariots and a great army there, and they came by night and surrounded the city. And when the servant of the man of God [Elisha] arose early and went out, there was an army, surrounding the city with horses and chariots. And his servant said to him, "Alas, my master! What shall we do?" . . . And Elisha prayed, and said, "LORD, I pray, open his eyes that he may see." Then the LORD opened the eyes of the young man, and he saw. And behold, the mountain was full of horses and chariots of fire all around Elisha. So when the Syrians came down to him, Elisha prayed to the LORD, and said, "Strike this people, I pray, with blindness." And He struck them with blindness according to the word of Elisha. (2 Kings 6:14–15, 17–18)

Elisha then led the blind army all the way to Samaria before their eyes were opened, again through the prayers of Elisha!

• *What new insights do you have into this passage of Scripture?*

_____

_____

Hedge Provided by a Righteous Person

At various places in the Bible, we find references made to those who "stood in the gap" or "stood in the breach" as being used by God to provide a defense for His righteous ones in the face of great danger or evil. Psalm 106:23 describes Moses as one such person who provided a wall of protection: "Therefore He said that He would destroy them, / Had not Moses His chosen one stood before Him in the breach, / To turn away His wrath, lest He destroy them."

The prophet Ezekiel gives this lament of the Lord: "'I sought for a man among them who would make a wall, and stand in the gap before Me on behalf of the land, that I should not destroy it; but

I found no one. Therefore I have poured out My indignation on them; I have consumed them with the fire of My wrath; and I have recompensed their deeds on their own heads,' says the Lord GOD" (Ezek. 22:30–31).

- *What new insights do you have into the power of prayer to protect your family from evil and also from God's judgment?*

_____

_____

Most of us do not experience this protective hedge formed by prayer for one simple reason: we do not pray with consistency and diligence for our families. What wondrous things we might see if we were to adopt a daily habit of praying diligently and fervently for those we love!

What Shall We Pray?

The Bible has a number of prayers that are appropriate for you to pray in behalf of your family. I recommend especially the prayer found in Colossians 1:9–14, which says,

For this reason we also, since the day we heard it [news of their faith in Jesus Christ, their love for the saints, and their love in the Spirit], do not cease to pray for you, and to ask that you may be filled with the knowledge of His will in all wisdom and spiritual understanding; that you may walk worthy of the Lord, fully pleasing Him, being fruitful in every good work and increasing in the knowledge of God; strengthened with all might, according to His glorious power, for all patience and longsuffering with joy; giving thanks to the Father who has qualified us to be partakers of the inheritance of the saints in the light. He has delivered us from the power of darkness and conveyed us into the kingdom of the Son of His love, in whom we have redemption through His blood, the forgiveness of sins.

• *What new insights do you have into this passage of Scripture?*

_____

_____

Let's take a closer look at four specific things Paul prays:

1. Wisdom and Spiritual Understanding About God's Will

Paul prays that the Colossians will be "filled with the knowledge of His will in all wisdom and spiritual understanding" (Col. 1:9). We are always in order to pray that we, as well as our family members, will know God's will for our lives. In a broad sense, knowing God's will is knowing your God-given talents and abilities, and then knowing how God would have you apply those talents to help others.

God desires that we have His wisdom about how to live our lives. Wisdom is highly practical—it is the knowledge of *how* to apply God's truths. God also desires that we have spiritual understanding, which is an understanding of how and why God does things the way He does them. Spiritual understanding is very close to discernment, which is the ability to see "behind the scenes" to the true motives for good or evil that are at work in any situation or relationship.

Ask God for His wisdom and spiritual understanding. Ask Him to reveal to you your purpose in living. Pray that your spouse and children might also know the reason for their creation, have greater wisdom in their daily decisions and choices, and be able to discern more clearly what it is that God is desiring to do in their lives.

What the Word Says	What the Word Says to Me
If any of you lacks wisdom, let him ask of God, who gives to all liberally and without reproach, and it will be given to him. But let him ask in faith, with no doubting. (James 1:5–6)	_____ _____ _____ _____ _____ _____
Now we have received, not the spirit of the world, but the Spirit who is from God, that we might	_____ _____ _____

know the things that have been
freely given to us by God. These
things we also speak, not in words
which man's wisdom teaches but
which the Holy Spirit teaches,
comparing spiritual things with
spiritual. (1 Cor. 2:12–13)

"Awake, you who sleep,
Arise from the dead,
And Christ will give you light."
See then that you walk circum-
spectly, not as fools but as wise,
redeeming the time, because the
days are evil. Therefore do not be
unwise, but understand what the
will of the Lord is." (Eph.
5:14–17)

2. Walking Worthy of the Lord

Paul prays that the Colossians may "walk worthy of the Lord,
fully pleasing Him, being fruitful in every good work and increasing in the knowledge of God" (Col. 1:10). The way to please God
is stated here very clearly: be fruitful in ministry to others and
develop an increasingly intimate relationship with God and His
Word. Surely that must be our prayer for ourselves, that we might
discover new and more effective ways to help others, that we might
have increasing insights into God's Word, and that we might have
an ever-deepening relationship with the Lord. We are never amiss
to pray this on behalf of our family members.

What the Word Says

I, therefore, the prisoner of the
Lord, beseech you to walk worthy
of the calling with which you were
called, with all lowliness and gentleness, with longsuffering,
bearing with one another in love,
endeavoring to keep the unity of

What the Word Says to Me

the Spirit in the bond of peace.
(Eph. 4:1–3)

Now may He who supplies seed
to the sower, and bread for food,
supply and multiply the seed you
have sown and increase the fruits of
your righteousness. (2 Cor. 9:10)

And this I pray, that your love may
abound still more and more in
knowledge and all discernment,
that you may approve the things
that are excellent, that you may be
sincere and without offense till the
day of Christ, being filled with the
fruits of righteousness which are
by Jesus Christ, to the glory and
praise of God. (Phil. 1:9–11)

For I desire mercy and not
sacrifice,
And the knowledge of God more
than burnt offerings. (Hos. 6:6)

He has shown you, O man, what
is good;
And what does the LORD require
of you
But to do justly,
To love mercy,
And to walk humbly with your
God? (Mic. 6:8)

3. Strengthened with All Might

Paul prays that the Colossians might be "strengthened with all might, according to His glorious power, for all patience and long-suffering with joy" (Col. 1:11). The kind of strength that Paul seeks on their behalf is *enduring* power—the ability to survive times of persecution and to remain steadfast in faith. This kind of strength comes as we draw our strength from the Lord, relying on Him fully to help us when we no longer can help ourselves. When we draw enduring power from the Lord, we also experience joy. We know that the Lord is helping us and that He is working on our behalf!

What gives us strength? Paul explains to the Ephesians that this kind of strength comes as we experience Christ's love—when we begin to understand how much God cares for us and actually "feel" His love welling up in our hearts. The person who is filled with love is a person who has *great* strength. What a wonderful thing to pray for your family, that each member of your family will be filled to overflowing with God's love!

What the Word Says

I know how to be abased, and I know how to abound. Everywhere and in all things I have learned both to be full and to be hungry, both to abound and to suffer need. I can do all things through Christ who strengthens me. (Phil. 4:12–13)

For this reason I bow my knees to the Father of our Lord Jesus Christ . . . that He would grant you, according to the riches of His glory, to be strengthened with might through His Spirit in the inner man, that Christ may dwell in your hearts through faith; that you, being rooted and grounded in love, may be able to compre- hend with all the saints what is the width and length and depth and height—to know the love of Christ which passes knowledge; that you may be filled with all the fullness of God. (Eph. 3:14, 16–19)

What the Word Says to Me

_____

_____

_____

_____

_____

_____

_____

_____

_____

_____

_____

_____

_____

_____

_____

_____

_____

_____

_____

_____

_____

_____

_____

_____

4. Thanksgiving for Our Salvation

Paul concludes his prayer for the Colossians by "giving thanks to the Father who has qualified us to be partakers of the inheritance of the saints in the light" (Col. 1:12). We, too, must offer praise and thanksgiving to God for our family members and, in particular, for their salvation. If members of your family are not saved, your number-one prayer for them should be that they will come to the point of receiving the forgiveness that God so freely and mercifully offers. If your family members are saved, then your prayer should be one of ongoing thanksgiving as well as a prayer that they will continue to walk in the light of the Holy Spirit.

What the Word Says	What the Word Says to Me
We give thanks to the God and Father of our Lord Jesus Christ, praying always for you. (Col. 1:3)	_____ _____ _____
I thank my God upon every remembrance of you, always in every prayer of mine making request for you all with joy, for your fellowship in the gospel from the first day until now, being confident of this very thing, that He who has begun a good work in you will complete it until the day of Jesus Christ. (Phil. 1:3–6)	_____ _____ _____ _____ _____ _____ _____ _____ _____
We give thanks to God always for you all, making mention of you in our prayers, remembering without ceasing your work of faith, labor of love, and patience of hope in our Lord Jesus Christ in the sight of our God and Father, knowing, beloved brethren, your election by God. . . . And you became followers of us and of the Lord, having received the word in much afflic-	_____ _____ _____ _____ _____ _____ _____ _____

tion, with joy of the Holy Spirit. (1
Thess. 1:2–4, 6)

_____
_____

Praying with Your Family

Not only can you use the prayer of Paul to the Colossians and
other prayers in the Bible as a part of your intercession for your
family members, but you can also pray these prayers *with your family members*. Let your children know what it is that you pray for
them. Let them hear you pray. Invite their prayers for you in return,
including a prayer that you will be the best parent possible.

Prayer is something that every person can do for his or her family. There is no excuse *not* to pray. God looks upon the intent and
love of your heart as you pray; you need never be concerned that
you aren't "using the right words."

Neither should you be concerned that you aren't praying in precisely the right way. If you are praying for the protection of God
against evil, and you are requesting strength and wisdom so that
your loved ones might withstand evil pressures, you are always praying for the right things. If you are praying out of love for your family
and out of a desire to see God work in their lives, you are praying
with the right motive.

When Paul described for the Ephesians how they were to don
the whole armor of God in doing spiritual battle, he concluded his
teaching by saying that those dressed for spiritual warfare should
be found "praying always with all prayer and supplication in the
Spirit" (Eph. 6:18). Pray for whatever it is that the Spirit prompts
you to pray for your family members. Pray often. Pray about every
situation, circumstance, relationship, and activity that involves your
family members.

Cover your family with prayer. And then trust God to cover them
with His protection.

- *What new insights do you have into how to pray for your family?*

_____

_____

- *In what ways do you feel challenged by the Holy Spirit today to pray for those you love?*

_____

_____

CONCLUSION

TRUST GOD TO DO WHAT ONLY GOD CAN DO

When you have done everything you know to do to protect your family from evil . . . when you have put into place the very best defense and offense against the devil that you know to establish . . . it is then time for you to trust God to act in the lives of your family members in the way only God can act.

Trust Him to convict your loved ones of sin.

Trust Him to save and heal your family members.

Trust Him to protect and provide for your children.

Trust Him to do what only God can do in any given circumstance.

You are not the "savior" of your family members, and neither are you their "lord." Jesus alone is Savior and Lord. Ultimately, we each must submit our life to God and follow Him out of our own volition.

I believe, however, that as you act and pray with faith, God will protect and provide, now and forever!